THE
CORPORATE
NEGAHOLIC

THE
CORPORATE
NEGAHOLIC

◆

How to Deal
Successfully with
Negative Colleagues,
Managers,
and Corporations

◆

◆ *Chérie Carter-Scott* ◆

Villard Books
NEW YORK
1991

Library of Congress Cataloging-in-Publication Data

Carter-Scott, Chérie.
Negaholics in the workplace / by Chérie Carter-Scott.
    p.   cm.
ISBN 0-394-58622-0
1. Psychology, Industrial. 2. Negativism.   I. Title.
HF5548.8.C238 1991   158.7—dc20   90-44466

Manufactured in the United States of America

9 8 7 6 5 4 3 2

FIRST EDITION

To Warren Bennis, who has believed in me and empowered me, who has been my mentor, my very special friend, and who has taught me the most about organizational development and life; to my dedicated partner and sister Lynn Stewart, who has been with me in the trenches every step of the way, and without whom the work could not have been possible; and to my daughter Jennifer, who loves me, supports me, and understands even when I can't be with her.

ACKNOWLEDGMENTS

I want to thank all those people who were brave and courageous enough to transcend their personal dysfunctions and undergo the process of organizational transformation, and also all those who contributed to the writing of this book: Velma Alexander, Carol Arenas, Mary Arguellas, Jim Autry, Pam Baker, Bill Battle, Sheila Barr, Kelly Barton, Brant Benun, Dan Bishop, Jaci Bodensteiner, Jerry Bogus, Kelly Bonner, Liz Brooks, Rain Burns, Nancy Byal, Mary Cajka, Sherry Camarillo, Christina Campbell, Denny Caringer, Chuck Carlson, Jim Carolan, Hugh Carpenter, Delois Carter-Leonard, Fred Chase, Dave Civian, Mary Conroy, Margaret Daly, Paul Dileo, Bob Dittmer, Brad Driggers, Doris Eby, Espie Ekman, Rosemary Ellis, Eva Erlacher, Michael Fontaine, Bob Furstenau, Rosemary Gardner, Jennifer Gerould, Steve Glick, Barbara Goldman, Dora Gomez, Kate Greer, Duane Gregg, Nancy Hall, Trish Hallier, Mic Hansen, Kathy Harris, Pam Harris, Trevor Harris, Bernie Heiler, Rachael Holincheck, Mebe Holmbe, Brad Hong, LeRoy Huff, Judy Hunsicker, Mark Ingebretsen, Tom Jackson, Beth Jandernoa, Andrew Jay, Sharon Jenkins, Doug Jimerson, Barbara Johnson, David Johnson, Lisa Johnson, David Jordan, Jack Joyce, Nancy Kluender, Paul Krantz, Jerry Kreger, Dennis Lam,

Robin Larkin, Kevin Ludgate, Gianna Maggiore, Dwane Marrioni, Pat Martin-Vegue, Tom Massey, Joan McCloskey, Sharon McGregor, Jan McKeon, William B. Milham, Dave Mitchell, Suzanne Mohr, Shawn Nadim, Bill Nolan, Ralph Odierna, Janet Padilla, Sherry Palmer, Diane Paulson, Marge Petty, Dolores Phipps, Lymon Pon, Jerry Preator, Jan Powell, Jerry Rank, Howard Rochestie, Sue Rodkey, Sue Russell, Tony Salgado, Joe Schlegel, Barbara Schugar, Norma Scriven, Jean T. Settlemyre, Jilann Severson, Susan Sheetz, Sandy Soria, Linda Thomas, Shirley Van Zante, Sarita Vargas, Frank Wagner, Jamie Weinstein, Mark Weiss, Marla Weiss, Colin Wheeler, Janice E. White, Trudy Wiley, Candy Williams, Dick Williams, Jim Williams, and Mardi Wood.

In particular I would like to thank Jim Stein, who is a blessing and a dear friend, and who is always there when I need him, as well as Diane Reverand, who is the best editor I can imagine.

CONTENTS

THE CLUES THAT CORPORATE NEGAHOLISM EXISTS • WHY IS THE SYNDROME CALLED "NEGAHOLISM"? • THE FOUR CATEGORIES OF CORPORATE NEGAHOLISM • ATTITUDINAL CORPORATE NEGAHOLICS • THE WORKAHOLIC WORKHORSE • THE CONSUMMATE CONTROLLER • THE POLITICAL PEACEMAKER • THE PERENNIAL EXPERT • BEHAVIORAL CORPORATE NEGAHOLICS • THE BLATANT BACK-STABBER • THE STATUS-QUO SUSTAINER • THE REBELLIOUS RABBLE-ROUSER • THE SOLITARY SUCCEEDER • MENTAL CORPORATE NEGAHOLICS • THE ERRATIC ECCENTRIC • THE MOROSE MELANCHOLIC • THE WALKING WOUNDED • VERBAL CORPORATE NEGAHOLICS • THE GARRULOUS GOSSIP • THE CHRONIC CYNIC • THE RESIGNED APATHETIC • SELF-SABOTAGE, OR SHOOTING YOURSELF IN THE FOOT

THE AVOIDER AND DENIER • THE TIME BOMB • THE ABUSIVE OGRE • THE DEMOTIVATING DRAGON • THE OVERWHELMING AVALANCHE • THE SPINELESS SAP • BATTLING BOSSES IN THE NEGA-TRENCHES

PART II
SITUATIONAL OR INTERDEPARTMENTAL
NEGAHOLISM

PART III
THE NEGAHOLIC CORPORATION

INTRODUCTION

This book is about a contagious corporate syndrome, corporate negaholism, that is sweeping the nation. It is about how corporate negaholism manifests itself daily in the lives of employees, managers, directors, and CEOs. In subtle ways, negative beliefs regarding the impossibility of extraordinary productivity, of teamwork between individuals and departments, and of providing outstanding customer service and satisfaction on the job can infect a majority of workers and drag an entire organization down to mediocrity, complacency, and in-fighting. Beliefs, attitudes, decisions, and perceptions that limit, reinforce the negative, and validate the impossible keep our organizations trapped in a holding pattern. Instead of moving forward into the desired future, we expend our energies motivating and managing negative employees, and negotiating between warring departments.

When you read this book, you will recognize people you know as victims of corporate negaholism. Not only will the case studies and examples seem familiar to you, but you will learn specific and tangible ways out of the corporate negaholic labyrinth. The tools and techniques outlined in this book will enable you to change old behavior patterns and create a healthy work environment.

I know this because I owned and managed my own negaholic corporation for fifteen years until I moved beyond my own dysfunctions and turned my organization around. I found ways to transcend the negaholic condition to which I was previously blind. The information I have gathered since then has not only helped thousands, but will be a great help to you as well.

In October 1974, I started a management-consulting business specializing in organizational development. I wasn't even familiar with organizational terminology yet, but I knew it had to do with visions, strategy, and empowerment.

Since 1974, my firm has consulted with small, medium, and large companies. We have worked with companies such as GTE/GTEL, AMI, Burger King, American Express, IBM, *Better Homes and Gardens*, Supercuts Franchises, Chevron USA, as well as thousands of midsize and smaller companies. Each ailing company is unique and deserves individual attention in order to shift its focus from dysfunction to full capacity.

My company offers process-oriented programs on team-building, managing organizational change and culture change, and excellence in customer service. We also offer content-oriented programs on interviewing skills, performance appraisal, communication skills, stress-management, time-management, sales training, presentation skills, and telephone courtesy. Over the years, it became clear that if the CEO or president of a corporation is willing to examine his vision, believe in it, map out a strategy, and enlist the support of the entire organization, incredible things can and do happen.

As a management consultant, I have witnessed such extraordinary positive changes in both individuals and in organizations that I felt compelled to write this book.

Turning a company around has far-reaching effects. The healing of old personal and interpersonal scars occurs on a very deep level; professionally, businesses become so functional that their profits are always significantly increased. Everyone benefits!

For example, we conducted a consulting project with the Burger King franchises in Wyoming. After six months, employee turnover dropped 81 percent in all four restaurants, management turnover dropped 96 percent, and net income system-wide increased 800 percent. This is what comes of eliminating negaholism in corporations.

Some of the questions which we ask top management are:

◆ What do you want in your professional life?
◆ What does your professional life look like now?
◆ What do you need to do to have your work situation utilize your abilities and skills, give you a sense of satisfaction, and reward you monetarily?
◆ What must happen to make your organization the way that you want it to be?
◆ What could possibly get in the way?

The process of turning a company around has three stages:

1. Determining the vision.
2. Strategizing the action plan.
3. Enlisting support in the realization of the vision.

There is a definite beginning, middle, and end to every business consulting assignment. We are not so much interested in the "why" or the "how" as the "what."

What do you want? What does it look like? What will it take? What do you need to do to get there? The process is solution-oriented and focuses on the realization of specific, tangible results.

Clients hire me because of my ability to focus, strategize, cut through to the essential issues, and pursue with them action plans that will bring about their desired futures.

These clients seek me out to:

- formulate visions, goals, and objectives.
- serve as a change agent.
- design a new curriculum.
- conduct team-building sessions among the management team.
- strategize action plans.
- facilitate meetings.
- resolve personnel issues from individual employee orientation to major culture change.
- clear up communication breakdowns between departments.
- act as a sounding board to solve problems.
- get an outside point of view on specific situations.
- provide individual consultations, group consultations, and interventions.
- recruit training specialists for specific needs.
- have a judgment-free environment in which to say anything.
- change old behavior patterns.
- help them design the next chapter in their professional lives.

The concept of corporate negaholism is the result of many years of research and trial and error. All the techniques in this book have been used by me and my clients to conquer corporate negaholism.

WHAT YOU WILL LEARN FROM THIS BOOK

This book has been written to help you:

♦ meet the "I can'ts" in your organization head-on without cringing.
♦ fortify the "I cans" in your organization and build them into a force to be reckoned with.
♦ ensure that the "I cans" run your organization.
♦ maintain a healthy organization.
♦ get what you want in your organization and in your life.

I hope the book is helpful to you in your professional life, and that you reap the benefits across the board. By the end of this book you will understand your company better and, most importantly, know how to change old habits and patterns and see your way through to the recovery process.

CHÉRIE CARTER-SCOTT

PART I

WHO ARE
THE CORPORATE
NEGAHOLICS?

CHAPTER 1

◆

IDENTIFYING
THE CORPORATE
NEGAHOLICS

It can't be done. There's no way. It's impossible. Do these phrases sound familiar? They are the earmarks of negaholism in the workplace. Corporate negaholism is a syndrome in which people unconsciously limit their own innate abilities, convince themselves that they can't have what they want, and sabotage not only their wishes, desires, and dreams, but those of the organization in which they work.

Corporate negaholics unconsciously bring personal negativity and dysfunctions dating from their childhoods to their work environment. When unrecognized and left unattended to, these same dysfunctions take over and begin to run the corporation itself. Eventually, the spread of dysfunctional behavior throughout the organization reaches epidemic proportions and becomes permanently ingrained, making it difficult to dis-

3

tinguish between the corporation itself and the subtle and insidious negaholism of the individuals who comprise it.

Corporate negaholics are everywhere. They are in the mail room, the marketing department, the accounting department, and on the front lines working with the public. They are secretaries, supervisors, managers, and directors. They exist alone or in small subgroups. Their negative attitudes and behaviors spread like a virus throughout the organization, contaminating the environment with workaholism, cynicism, and general malaise.

I have coined the word "negaholism" to describe a condition that may exist systematically in an organization, both interdepartmentally and in specific people. The world abounds in negaholic companies and people. Over and over again, I have seen people bring their individual dysfunctions from their family of origin into the work environment, where they reenact old patterns and problems with newly-assigned work associates, or "siblings."

THE CLUES THAT CORPORATE NEGAHOLISM EXISTS

Corporate negaholism exists when:

◆ people's behavior is motivated out of a desire to protect themselves, each other, or to preserve the status quo rather than fulfill the mission of the organization.

◆ people's individual compulsions, addictions, and neuroses begin to dominate and determine the strategy, activities, and even the direction of the company.

◆ individuals turn the negativity they feel about themselves toward the organization that employs them.

◆ employees spend the majority of their time criticizing or judging their co-workers, the management of the organization, the policies, or the way things are being done instead of taking constructive action.

◆ employees act out the sentiment, "Why would I want to be part of an organization that would have me as an employee?"

◆ individuals unconsciously work out their unresolved childhood issues (i.e., the pursuit of attention, recognition, approval, love, sibling rivalry, rebellion against authority figures, etc.) with their families in a work environment.

◆ the self-sabotage that individuals personally experience is transferred to the organization.

◆ dysfunctional behavior contaminates the employees, who in turn infect the customers, which seriously affects the bottom line.

◆ the "I can'ts" have taken over through a long, slow process, inculcating the majority of employees in such a way that they have become addicted to their own negativity.

◆ there is no consequence-management, and therefore no incentive for individuals to strive for excellence and make a difference.

Ask yourself these questions:

◆ Do you or your associates feel a lack of enthusiasm when you think of going into the office?

- Do you dread the idea of dealing with internal politics one more time?
- Do you try to avoid certain individuals so that you just don't have to deal with the frustration of interacting with them?
- Are you tired of inconsistencies in an office where direction, strategy, policy, or procedures can change from day to day?
- Are certain philosophies and attitudes lauded but in actuality not practiced?
- When a new program is initiated, do people think, "This too will pass"?
- Do you find yourself looking forward to retirement and biding your time until then?
- Do the budgetary cuts make absolutely no sense?
- Do you or others feel that you simply can't make a difference, no matter how hard you try?

WHY IS THE SYNDROME CALLED "NEGAHOLISM"?

A negaholic is one who is addicted to negativity. *Negare* is a Latin verb meaning "to deny." The "I can'ts" deny that the "I cans" possess any innate capability to change things for the better. Denying means that the "I can'ts" refuse to accept the fact that the "I cans" are capable, competent, and able to have what they want. The "I can'ts" deny that the "I cans" are worthy, lovable, and deserving.

Who are the corporate negaholics? How can you recognize them?

A corporate negaholic is one who is victimized by inner forces which manifest themselves through various negative attitudes, thoughts, words, or behaviors.

Corporate negaholics unconsciously sabotage not only their own actions, but those of their co-workers and the mission of the organization.

Wayne is a good example. The following three office scenarios with Wayne illustrate the different degrees of negaholism and their manifestations.

Scenario 1:

Wayne is upset. "Marla is out again for one of her two-hour lunches, Sam is fraternizing with the staff again, and I can't get accurate information out of the data processing department." He stomps around the office, muttering curses. It is clear to the staff members that they had better stay out of his way. This is not an exceptionally bad day for Wayne, since he is upset much of the time. He knows he is upset, and he considers his condition normal. He believes that the degree to which he is upset shows how much he really cares about the office, his staff, and the company in general. He honestly thinks that his condition is a direct result of the actions of his co-workers. He had no idea that his discomfort stems from frustration and an inability to deal successfully with any given situation. He resigns himself to simply working harder so that he can feel some sense of accomplishment. His belief is that if he can control his actions and get some results, then he will have a good day, albeit a frustrating one.

Scenario 2:

Wayne has the same problems as in the first scenario, but this time he is aware of some chattering in his head, a critical voice accusing him of handling things badly with Marla, and blaming him for Sam's indiscretions. He is aware of his feelings of anger and exasper-

7

ation, and decides to call a confidant: the company consultant.

Scenario 3:

Wayne becomes erratic and obsessed with the problems in the office. He is tormented by the screaming meanies in his head. "You should have sat down with Marla ages ago and told her right out that the two-hour lunches have to stop. You were irresponsible with her. If you're going to be a successful branch manager, you'd better get things straightened out now. I can't believe you've let it go so long! By ignoring her actions, you've tacitly allowed Marla to continue them. That whole situation with Sam is an embarrassment. Everyone talks about him behind his back, and he manages the largest department. If you can't get your employees to respect the management around here, you'll never be effective. And as for the data processing department, when are you ever going to get results from those guys? You simply can't get the information that you want when you need it. It's ridiculous that a company of this size operates with a pathetic data processing department. You had one too many scotches last night. You have to deal with Davey, who got picked up for smoking marijuana last week. Really, what *can* you do right?"

Wayne's feelings have escalated from concern to intense anxiety. He is bordering on a full-fledged neg-attack.

In these three examples we see the different levels of corporate negaholism. In the first scenario, Wayne has a moderate case of corporate negaholism and a rather limited awareness of his condition. In the second scenario, his condition is actually less serious, and the solution is to reach out to a safe, empathetic person for support. By reaching out, Wayne displays a reasonable amount of self-awareness, and at least admits that he is not perfect and needs some help. In the third scenario, Wayne is in very bad shape. He has become morbidly self-absorbed. The "I can'ts" have taken over and are totally in charge. They are beating him about the head and shoulders with not only how he didn't, and how he shouldn't have, but how he couldn't as well.

There are a myriad of subtle and sneaky ways that personal dysfunctions slip into your work life. Let's take a closer look at each type.

THE FOUR CATEGORIES OF CORPORATE NEGAHOLISM

I have separated corporate negaholics into four categories so that you can see how all-pervasive the syndrome is, and how many different forms it assumes. After having seen every form of corporate negaholism over the past seventeen years, I have been able to assign them their appropriate labels and group them into specific categories. It's difficult to distinguish one type of corporate negaholic from another, but I have assigned labels to the different types based upon their most blatant characteristics. One category often spills over into the next, but the negative attitudes and thoughts of each category are distinguishable through typical words and actions.

Attitudinal Corporate Negaholics are deeply dissatisfied people. On a very deep level they believe that it is not possible to ever really enjoy work. Either they set a standard which is impossible to live up to, or they can never do enough, be good enough, or have enough to satisfy the relentless demon which drives them.

Attitudinal corporate negaholics are successful people who drive themselves relentlessly. To the outsider they appear to have it all together, but inside they are driven and tormented. This is the most subtle form of negaholism because on the surface all is perfect: clean, orderly, aesthetically pleasing, and controlled. The negaholics in this group are: The Workaholic Workhorse, The Consummate Controller, The Political Peacemaker, and The Perennial Expert. The reason I have grouped these four into the attitudinal set is because their common bond is an all-pervasive negative attitude which dictates their negaholic behaviors.

Behavioral Corporate Negaholics can be similar to attitudinal negaholics in that they are often successful, but their tragic flaw is that they have one or more behaviors which keep them from achieving their objectives. Sometimes they succeed in spite of themselves, but most often they miss the mark. They try hard, but self-sabotage is written all over their actions. Caught in the discrepancy between their ideas and their actions, they constantly try but are unable to break out of their behavior patterns. This group consists of: The Blatant Back-stabber, The Status-Quo Sustainer, The Rebellious Rabble-rouser, and The Solitary Succeeder.

Behavioral corporate negaholics often act out their negativity in personally destructive ways, such as compulsion with work, isolation, smoking, overeating, excessive drinking either on or off the job, abuse of drugs which affect work performance, overindulgence in gossiping, colluding, wasting time, or playing practical jokes on colleagues.

Mental Corporate Negaholics are constantly flogging

themselves for something. They obsess about something they have said or done, lock onto the unforgettable, act and rub salt in the wound forever. Through criticism, invalidation, judgments, and mental abuse, they ruthlessly blame themselves for the past, the present, or the future. The Erratic Eccentric, The Morose Melancholic, and The Walking Wounded are all grouped as mental corporate negaholics because their mental harangues run their lives and drive their behaviors.

Verbal Corporate Negaholics say negative things about themselves, others, situations, places, and just about anything. Incredibly enough, they haven't the slightest idea that they are being negative, and think instead that they are accurately reporting the facts the way they are. In this group are: The Garrulous Gossip, The Chronic Cynic, and, of course, The Resigned Apathetic. The most obvious characteristic of verbal corporate negaholics is that they display their negaholism through their negative conversations. After a conversation with a verbal corporate negaholic, you will invariably feel less inspired, less enthusiastic, and less hopeful than you did before.

ATTITUDINAL CORPORATE NEGAHOLICS

The Workaholic Workhorse is a blend of good news and bad news. The workaholic looks like the ideal employee on the outside. He appears to be devoted, loyal, and willing to do whatever is needed and wanted. He arrives early, stays late, and often comes in on weekends. His life is devoted to his job, and he seems to like it that way. He has a great sense of pride in his dedication—almost bordering on obsession—to his work. In effect, he is married to his job, and appears to be fulfilled. Why then would a workaholic in a corporation be considered a negaholic?

Olivia is a genuine Workaholic Workhorse. She is competent, poised, and commands respect. That she can be counted on is a given. If you want a job done, done right, and done ahead of schedule, you should ask Olivia to do it. Her dedication to the corporation is unquestionable. She comes in at seven, stays late, will sacrifice dinner with her understanding husband when there is an emergency at the office, and on weekends can frequently be seen completing paperwork. She knows her priorities, and lunch is not high on the list. On weekends she runs a church group, and two nights a week she takes real estate classes. She loves her job and is revered by her co-workers. Her job is her life. She will never complain, has little to no social life, and has chosen not to have children. After six months of intense work, she is at the point of physical breakdown and usually needs a week off to recuperate. Though everyone's confidante, she loses sight of any balance in her own life. Since she runs herself into the ground, later she has to pick up the pieces and regroup. She has difficulty knowing what her personal boundaries are, and cannot effectively differentiate between herself and her job. At times she thinks she *is* her job. Since she gets a great deal of reinforcement from her boss and her co-workers, Olivia feels loved, respected, trusted, and appreciated in her professional role. The more she does, the more she is validated, and the more she wants to do, the more she commits to do.

Olivia's workaholism began with her family of origin. She was the fourth child in a very religious family of ten children. She rarely received attention or recognition; in fact, she felt invisible. Her role was to be the "good child" who got straight A's, was quiet, kept out of the way, and always helped mother with the younger children. She was super responsible and well behaved. Olivia was simply expected to be perfect. When she entered corporate life, Olivia continued to play the good child. In the corporate environment, her behavior was appreciated and reinforced with praise, recognition, and rewards. Olivia was initially timid and shocked by the response. She didn't know what to do with the onslaught of positive reinforcement. After a while, though, she began to enjoy the positive attention and look for more. The more reinforcement she received, the harder she would work, and so on.

The Consummate Controller needs to control everyone and everything within his domain. He needs to make sure that things are done right. Being done right almost always means done his way, the right way. The good news is that you will usually get top-quality work from the Consummate Controller. The bad news is that it is difficult if not impossible to be a creative, expressive individual around him. He knows the best way to do everything and is uninterested in your good ideas. He knows what he wants: simply put, it's "Do it my way." If you must master a technical task which needs to be done one way and one way only, he is a terrific teacher, but keep him away from situations in which there is room for individual self-expression.

The obvious question is, "How is he a corporate negaholic?" In the presence of the Consummate Controller, there is very little opportunity to develop as an individual or to grow. Since there is his way and only his way, teamwork is not possible, nor is the opportunity to come up with an original thought or solution. His need for control, his dysfunction, is running his department as well as his life.

Royce, the verbally abusive president of an automotive company, refuses to delegate and dwells on how everyone around him does everything wrong. After twenty-seven years of experience on the job, he is considered the best in the field. A perfectionist by nature, he has no tolerance for mistakes. He wants everything done right, so much so that he is willing to do whatever is needed himself. He has little patience for beginners, is uninterested in educating anyone, and begins to roar like a lion when he finds inaccuracies. He rarely gives praise. People live in fear of his outbursts, and retaliate covertly by ridiculing him behind his back.

Royce came from a very poor family. He recalls that there were times when he went without shoes because his parents couldn't afford them. He spent very little time in school, and completely dropped out when he was twelve years old in order to help his father with his work. His father always told him, "Royce, if you're going to make anything of your life, you have to do it yourself. Nobody is going to give it to you. It's up to you. Nobody really cares at all, so if you want something, go out and get it!"

Royce had his father's words emblazoned on his frontal lobes. After working for a time with his father, at the age of fifteen he got a paying job and went back to school. He knew intuitively that an education was important, so he worked doubly hard at learning how to read, spell, and add. By the age of eighteen he had completed high school, and started work in the automotive industry. While he worked during the day, he took courses at City College in the evenings. He got his B.A. and succeeded at everything he attempted. He made his father's words a reality.

Royce's story is inspiring, except for the fact that he now expects from everyone else the same degree of commitment that he himself exhibited. He is relentless, intolerant, and compassionless. His style is unreasonable and abusive. What worked for Royce in his personal life works against him in his professional life. People have to work around him, and no one dares broach the subject of his management style. He is defensive and righteous, but his skill in his field makes his position almost unassailable. Certainly he is respected and revered, but it has cost him a lot.

The Political Peacemaker has learned how to dress, whom to talk to when, and whom to compliment. He has the game figured out. Each day for him means engaging in a larger-than-life chess game in which he strategizes every move and plays to win. He is keen in his observations, and knows who has the power and who holds the purse strings. He employs situational ethics, manipulates people for his personal gain, and says and does whatever will get him what he wants.

Nate, a successful sales manager in his early forties, is a veritable political animal. He watches to see which way the current is flowing and moves with it. He has no real biases, opinions, or passions, since his sole commitment is to his own personal gain. He has learned how to behave through observation, and immediately exploits the information he absorbs. His employees regard him with disdain and resentment. Through intimidation, he keeps the operation going. He acts busy, surly, and preoccupied. He is unavailable to his staff emotionally, interpersonally, or managerially. He plays with the upper echelon to the exclusion of his staff. Nate was the middle child in a family of three boys. His older brother, Jake, was always under scrutiny, and his younger brother, Drew, continually got away with murder. Nate's family was extremely emotive. His parents were demonstrative with both affection and violence. His mother had been an affection-starved child who developed into an incurable flirt. She only experienced validation through male attention. As a result, Nate's father would become violently jealous every time Annabelle, Nate's mother, invited a man's advances. It was rumored that Annabelle had numerous affairs, but no one knew for sure.

Given the intense drama, the open expression of emotion, and the turbulent and inconsistent climate of his family life, Nate adopted the role of the "peacemaker" and learned early on how to calm the turbulent waters. Nate learned to tell people what they wanted to hear in order to keep peace in the house. He felt it was his responsibility to maintain harmony. No one else was doing that job, it needed to be done, and Nate appointed himself to the task. He believed that the violence put everyone at risk and that he needed to be responsible for keeping everyone alive. Nate would placate his father by denying that his mother was flirting. He would tell his mother that his father's violent outbursts were indicative of the degree of love he felt for her. He would agree with Jake, telling him that he was right and that his parents were wrong. He would coddle Drew in a gentle, positive way, encouraging him to do whatever he wanted and covering for him in his absence. He did not think of himself as lying, but rather as keeping the peace. He felt absolute license to tell anyone anything that would alleviate tension in the home. In professional life, Nate would invariably be drawn to exciting, dramatic, chaotic environments where he could feel "at home," and there he would exercise his peacemaking skills in much the same way he had as a boy. As long as he kept the different coalitions separate, he was safe to continue his game and carry out his childhood pattern.

The Perennial Expert is overly impressed with his own importance. He always assumes the position of the expert. He seldom asks questions, but rather assumes the posture of the all-knowing expert on almost every subject.

Harry got his law degree from an Ivy League college, and he'll never let you forget it. If you didn't know better, you'd think he spent all of his time reading wine books, newspapers, magazines, history texts, and trivia collections. It's not that he is so smart, but just that he always has an answer to every question. It would be a surprise to hear him say, "I don't know." With one hand in his pocket, he struts arrogantly around his office while dictating to his secretary. His tone has a note of condescension to it. He uses eye-rolling, sighing, and clucking to nonverbally communicate his displeasure. Neophytes are impressed, the well-seasoned tolerate him with boredom, and the old veterans dismiss him as a relic in the corporate trophy room.

Harry's father was a judge, and his three brothers became attorneys, just like Harry. There was always intense competition between Harry and his brothers over just about everything. They were competitive over knowledge of baseball scores, running races, skiing, tennis, grades in school, popularity with girls, their mother's attention, money; you name it, they could feel competitive over it. Harry was the oldest, and he felt unrelenting pressure to be the best. After all, he was the tallest, the biggest, and the oldest, and he naturally felt he was looked to as the one who needed to set the tone for the others.

The competition that Harry experienced in early childhood developed into his need as an adult to be "right" in everything he said and did. Harry felt a strong compulsion to be the best, to know more, and to have done more things better than anyone else. He was driven to be smarter, faster, stronger, and better informed than anyone else. He felt deep down that his very survival depended upon it. Harry felt that if he wasn't the best in something, he would be found out and deemed completely worthless. Being second best was not an option. Only the very best was acceptable, and that was expected.

In childhood, Harry earned kudos for his outstanding record, but as he drifted into adulthood, his inability to work with others became quite noticeable. Harry finally left the computer company in which he was corporate counsel, and started his own law firm. His reason was that his former colleagues were lightweights who were jealous of his success. His colleagues had a different story: they were tired of playing winners and losers with someone who was supposed to be on the same team.

BEHAVIORAL CORPORATE NEGAHOLICS

You tend to feel sorry for behavioral negaholics. They trip themselves up time and time again. They appear to be "hooked" on their behavior and unable to stop what they are doing. They are often sweet people whom you want to help. If you come into contact with them, behavioral corporate negaholics will seduce you and possibly get you to invest more in their problems than they are doing themselves. The four types of behavioral negaholics are: The Blatant Back-Stabber, The Status Quo Sustainer, The Rebellious Rabble-Rouser, and The Solitary Succeeder.

The Blatant Back-stabber finds her specialty in saying the wrong thing at the wrong time to the wrong person. She is completely unaware that her co-workers take offense at her cattiness, her put-downs, and her covert hostility. She'll say one thing to your face and another behind your back, and then the word gets out: Don't trust her! You can't tell her anything without it being used against you. Watch out for her, she's trouble!

Glenda shoots herself in the foot every time she is up for promotion. The top marketing person in her firm, her reputation is that she can close any deal, and her clients love her. Her tragic flaw is that she cannot get along with her co-workers. She talks about anyone and everyone in deprecating terms when they are not present. She cannot understand why her career is going nowhere. Management vacillates between love and hate for Glenda, and generally is at a loss as to what to do with her. Professionally speaking, she is her own worst enemy.

Glenda was raised by her mother, who was struggling to make ends meet as a single parent. Abandoned by her husband, Rosalie faced the world with a chip on her shoulder. Her resentment spread to everything she

19

did. Since Glenda was her only child, she got an earful of her mother's complaints. As a child she was powerless to change her situation, and was forced to listen to her mother's endless harangues. Rosalie would maintain a perpetual commentary on everyone, male or female, acquaintance or stranger. Rosalie's critiques were indiscriminate, and friend and foe alike came under her fire.

Glenda grew up believing that this behavior was normal. She contracted her negaholism from her mother, and without any awareness that a running monologue riddled with judgments and criticisms was not desirable, she perpetuated the tradition. Her personal life wasn't seriously impaired, but when she entered the publishing field, she was in for some new reactions.

Glenda had two antithetical aspects to her personality. First, she was a top-notch producer. Second, she would talk about everyone, including her so-called allies and friends, behind their backs, in the same judgmental and deprecating way that her mother had. Her personal dysfunction, learned through example, became her professional nemesis.

The Status-Quo Sustainer is a peacemaker to the point of denying or ignoring that anything is ever wrong. A classic nonconfrontationalist, the status quo sustainer avoids friction at all costs. This person is more concerned about peace and harmony than about truth, honesty, solutions, or results.

Dottie marches through the office with a drill sergeant's determination. She ploughs through her projects with a vengeance, and handles her staff with little sensitivity.

Alice walked into Dottie's office with an anxious look on her face. "The staff is unhappy with the decision which you made about the future of the newspaper," she said. "They're upset that they had no input in the decision. Some of them are putting together their résumés and are seriously considering going elsewhere."

Dottie looked surprised and sympathetic. "Now dear, they'll get over it. I can't imagine that they're upset. It didn't take a summit meeting to make that decision. They've known it was coming all along. There is really nothing to be upset about!"

"Well, they're not happy with things the way they are. We've really got a hornet's nest on our hands. Whether you like it or not, this is a big one," Alice stated matter-of-factly.

"Now there there, with a little time they'll get over it. Don't you worry about a thing. If people are upset, you just tell them to come and see me. It'll all be just fine. Why don't you and Jim go to a movie tonight? I hear the one playing at the Roxy is hysterical. Do something nice for yourself," Dottie said condescendingly.

Exasperated and crestfallen, Alice left Dottie's office feeling hopeless. Alice wanted to resolve the undercurrent of conflict in the office, but Dottie was unwilling to grasp the severity of the situation.

Dottie's childhood had little to no consistency. Her father had been in the military, and had moved the family at least once a year. Her mother was emotionally unstable and took tranquilizers to control her moods. There were five children, and the father ran the house as if he were issuing orders to his troops. Dottie learned how to survive in the midst of all of the chaos. She made an unconscious decision to act as the ballast in the family structure. Her commitment was to bring order to the chaos, to still the troubled waters, and to be cheerful in the midst of trauma. Maintaining the status quo was her deepest desire, and her primary objective in all situations.

When Dottie came to the newspaper, she was cheerful and pleasant, efficient and orderly. She conducted herself as a competent professional. She was punctual and prepared. Her personal dysfunction of maintaining the status quo, however, soon became apparent in her inability to confront or directly deal with any unpleasant situation. Her need to gloss over, make nice, and deny the reality of the situation compounded her professional dysfunctions. Upper management didn't see that Dottie had a problem, but her direct subordinates did. They felt unable to come to her with unpleasant situations or difficulties because she simply refused to deal with them.

The Rebellious Rabble-rouser is frequently moody and often upset. He feels frustrated with how to effect results in the system. Incompetency and inefficiency aggravate him and, with his lack of people skills and his clumsy attempts at communication, he frequently alienates those around him. He is a powder keg who could ignite at the slightest provocation. His tales are full of anecdotes about morons, idiots, and buffoons who recently said and/or did the world's stupidest thing. He is obsessed with bucking the system at other people's expense.

Seth likes to maintain eye contact until you glance away. Exceptionally bright, talented, and quick, he can always pinpoint what needs to happen to make a project work. Seth is the art director of a major advertising agency. He is respected in his field, but everyone steers

clear of him. His interpersonal skills are those of a Neanderthal, and he steps on people's toes, in the cause of
aestheticism, without even knowing it. Hurting people's feelings is his modus operandi, and he does it
quite innocently. He is a maverick who somehow ended
up in a corporation.

Seth acts like he is in prison, seeking ways to express himself, and feeling thwarted at every turn. He is
caught between his brilliance and his clumsiness, between his solitariness and his need to function as part of
a team, and between his need for autonomy and his
niche in the corporate world. When you talk to him you
can sense anger and hostility, and yet you don't know
what lies behind it. He seems about to explode, but he
keeps himself neatly in check.

Seth was raised in a small town in the Midwest. He
was a gifted child who felt misunderstood and ridiculed
for his brilliance. He spent much of his childhood alone,
drawing, brooding, and feeling different. He felt as if
his parents didn't understand him. He spent a lot of
time explaining himself to his teachers. He labored
through the teasing of his peers, and he found solace in
the company of animals. He thought for years that he
might become a veterinarian, but his outstanding artistic ability determined his future.

Early on, Seth decided that the world was a hostile
place. He decided that, in order to survive, he had to
take care of himself and guard himself against a cruel
world. He was blessed with talents that seemed like a
curse to him. He didn't fit in, and he never would. His
socialization process was arrested at a very young age
and had never recovered.

As an adult, Seth was like a very tall seven-year-old
trapped in a grown-up's body. He wanted to be in-

cluded, accepted, and loved just like any other person, but the deep hurts from his past, which had inhibited his emotional development, prevented this. He found himself the art director of a major advertising agency, yet he was afraid of and unskilled at relating to others. He had a staff of eight people who looked to him for direction, and yet all they received was criticism, neglect, and suppressed hostility. The dysfunctions created by his early experiences affected his performance as a businessman.

The Solitary Succeeder is extremely capable in task-management on his own, but is unable to work with others as a team. He knows he can count on himself, but he does not trust others and refuses to rely on them to get the job done. His scope is limited to what he can accomplish by himself. Sometimes these feats are truly Herculean, but always limited by what he himself can effect. Others regard him with respect for his discipline, his positive energy, and his abilities, but also with disdain because he is isolated.

Gavin is the director of operations for a large computer firm. There isn't a technical job which he can't do. He trusts himself, his hands, his brain, and his problem-solving abilities, but that's where the trust stops. He doesn't trust anyone else. He doesn't think that anyone can do the job as well as he can. Over and over again, he proves this self-fulfilling prophesy. He ends up doing every job by himself. Whether it's been delegated or not, somehow or other each project ends up back in his lap.

"I knew I'd end up doing this job myself," is his oft-repeated complaint. His manager worries about

Gavin's future. Since he is so capable, there are a myriad of possibilities open to him, but since he lacks the ability to work with others, his options rapidly become limited. His rigidity and righteousness keep him trapped in a box labeled "Star, do not touch!"

Gavin has two distinct sides to his personality. He has the charming, sweet, and endearing side which is willing and eager to help a friend with any task. The other side of him is cold, distant, and cruel. Most people know only his warm and friendly public side, but those who get close to him discover his dark side. It's astonishing to realize that both of these characters live in the same body. The cold, biting, sardonic Gavin can in fact be vicious if he feels threatened. Perhaps the reason that he isolates himself is to protect this side and to keep others from seeing it. By working alone, he doesn't have to risk rejection through discovery.

The split in Gavin is a clear reflection of the split between his parents. His mother was a kind, sweet, unconditionally loving mother who made him feel right no matter what, and who worshipped the ground he walked on. His father, on the other hand, was critical and judgmental. Nothing Gavin ever did was quite good enough. His father would pick apart anything he accomplished by continually telling him how he could improve it or how he should have done it differently.

Gavin felt whole and complete around his mother and totally worthless around his father. Since his father traveled a great deal for his work, Gavin felt valued most of the time. However, every three months, when his father came home, he would get a dose of "You're not good enough!" which made up for the father's prolonged absence. As an adult, Gavin never integrated the attitudes of his mother and father. If he kept other people away, he would never have to deal with the criticism and judgments which they might offer, and he could harbor the nurturing mother who loved everything he did. As an adult, Gavin was determined to succeed. Succeed he did, but he did it alone.

MENTAL CORPORATE NEGAHOLICS

Perhaps the most subtle and insidious form of negaholism is mental. Sometimes you will be completely unaware of your own thoughts. You may begin to feel low, withdrawn, or in a funk, and have no idea why. Mental negaholics often transfer their thoughts into negaholic actions. There are, however, mental negaholics who live exclusively in their own private world of self-inflicted punishment. The Erratic Eccentric, The Morose Melancholic, and The Walking Wounded are all different types of mental negaholics.

The Erratic Eccentric is either up and hyper or down and out. Binary is his middle name. He rarely takes the middle path, and is either ecstatic or depressed. He is inconsistent and hard to read. You always have to be on your toes around him because he's so unpredictable. You're not sure if it's hormones, moods, or chemicals, but his changeability could drive you crazy. You must match his moods or you'll incur his wrath.

You'd think Trent were on drugs if you didn't know him better. One hour he is up, and then something happens which upsets him and he's down in the dumps. If you made a graph of his moods it would look like a series of intense highs followed by equally gripping lows. To be around him is like being in a melodrama that has no intermission. His staff checks first to see if this is a "good" day or a "bad" day, and then acts accordingly.

Trent came from a family of all boys. His mother was overprotective and his father ignored him. His family life was full of highs and lows. When Randall, the father, had landed a big deal, the whole family would celebrate and everyone was happy. When times were rough, the heavy drinking and fighting would begin. The mood swings were intense and life was largely inconsistent. Affection was also given and taken away at will, with little or no explanation. At one moment his mother would be loving, at another she could change and without warning become extremely nasty.

Trent grew up in an erratic environment which he believed was "normal." The lack of predictability became deeply enmeshed in his behavior patterns, so that as an adult he operated in the same way that his family of origin had. He never considered that his behavior was difficult for those around him, since he perceived himself as normal, healthy, and well-adjusted.

Trent's mood swings affected his entire office. In a series of interviews, his employees began complaining about his lack of consistency. They were uncertain and didn't know what to expect. They felt uneasy with the lack of predictability. When his behavior patterns were brought to his attention, Trent was shocked and became eager to change his behavior.

The Morose Melancholic feels that it hasn't worked, it doesn't work, and it never will work. "Life is tough, and you have to work to pay the bills. You're never going to like your job, so just do any old thing, take the

27

money, and go home. There is no way out, you're trapped. Stop fighting it and accept the fact that it's going to be like this for the rest of your life." This sounds like chronic depression, and in fact the only difference is that depression is a clinical condition and morose melancholy is a way of perceiving life. Hopeless, helpless, unable to change themselves, their situation, or their behavior, morose melancholics live with sadness and resentment.

Thelma punches in and punches out. She does her job and goes home. Her work is joyless drudgery from paycheck to paycheck. She views her life as going nowhere, with only dead ends ahead of her. She'd like to change, venture out, start her own business, or team up with a partner, but she's too scared to break out of her mold. Caught in the no-man's land between what she wants and the enemy within who says she can't have it, she feels absolutely paralyzed and chronically unhappy.

Thelma was raised by her mother and her grandmother. Her mother had three children, a boy and two girls. Thelma was the oldest and was expected to be a boy. When she wasn't, both parents were disappointed, the father because he wanted an heir and the mother because she had failed by giving him a girl. From the moment of Thelma's birth, she felt as if she weren't good enough, as if she'd failed, as if who she was were not enough. Her father left the family after the birth of her little brother, which made her mother feel like a failure. Her bitterness spread to the children, and her daughters had no doubt that men were mean and evil creatures who only wanted to use them and discard them once they'd had their pleasure. At forty-five, Thelma was still a virgin. She probably always would be, given her early imprinting.

Thelma brought her sadness, her hopelessness, and her despair to her job. Since she was excellent at task-management, she was promoted to supervising twenty-seven women. She found the pressure of interacting with so many different personality types unbearable. She had never learned how to manage relationships. She felt inadequate, and thought the only way to succeed was to do nice things for her staff. She spent almost all of her free time baking cookies, knitting sweaters, sewing Christmas stockings, and buying birthday presents. It was a full-time job keeping twenty-seven people happy, and most of the time she felt burdened and exhausted.

The Walking Wounded does just what is required, tries not to make waves, stays out of the way, and behaves himself, all the while living a mouse-like existence. Doing whatever he can not to be noticed, either because of a past incident, a physical handicap, an emotional trauma, a mental impairment, insecurity, fear of people, or chronic shyness, he stays out of the line of fire and gets the job done without attracting attention. He has little to no ambition in life, since his spark was snuffed out long ago.

Alan lost his family suddenly in a car accident seven years ago. All were killed, his wife and two children. Alan was not with them the day they were driving back from vacation because he had to return to his job early. After the accident, something snapped inside him. He's never been the same since. He smiles a lot, but you never know whether it's genuine or glued on as a part of the role he is playing in the corporate drama. He does his job well, but everyone walks on eggshells around him so as not to upset him. People talk about him behind his back in sympathetic, hushed voices. Each year he gets his seven percent cost of living increase and a pat on the back. He has no friends, no career path, and his future looks pretty much the same as the present. He does what he's supposed to do, nobody gets upset, and nobody bothers him. Actually, everybody for the most part ignores him. He doesn't take up much space and he minds his own business.

Alan was one of eight children in an immigrant family. His family had come over from Italy to make a new life for themselves. His father was the patriarch who ruled the roost, and his mother lovingly raised the brood. Alan learned as a boy to be a good person, to go to church, and to support and care for his family. He would find his reward in heaven. For twelve years, Alan did exactly what his parents would have wanted.

When the tragedy struck, Alan's world shattered. He could never forgive himself for letting his wife and children drive home without him. His sin was so heinous and so unforgivable that he snapped. He walked around with such a deep sense of shame that he couldn't face anyone. In the office he was tolerated and pitied, but people worked around him. No one dared talk to him except to say, "Hi, how are you?" He would always say "fine," and that was that.

VERBAL CORPORATE NEGAHOLICS

A verbal negaholic is someone you can't get far enough away from. Listening to one can either trigger your own latent negaholism or just drive you crazy. Focusing on the negative by highlighting the worst-case scenarios is his full-time preoccupation. Unless you maintain your sense of humor, being around a verbal negaholic can be very depressing. There are three types of verbal negaholics: **The Garrulous Gossip, The Chronic Cynic,** and **The Resigned Apathetic.**

Verbal negaholics look at life as if it were the proverbial half-empty glass as opposed to the half-full one. Their prevailing attitude is that they need to protect themselves, and to expect the worst. "Life is tough," "Wouldn't you know it would happen to me," and "It's just my luck" are famous quotes from verbal negaholics. Since these beliefs underlie all their words and actions, it is understandable that these negaholics would need to prove themselves right. The way their lives unfold is totally appropriate to their beliefs.

The Garrulous Gossip chatters non-stop and drives the office crazy. The polar opposite of the Walking Wounded, she is in constant need of attention. She never stops prattling on about the latest piece of gossip, and imparts confidential information indiscriminately. It's difficult to discount her as a person since she is helpful and competent. She is efficient and capable of getting almost anything done, but her nervousness and insecurity keep her talking endlessly. Her secret scoops make her feel incredibly intelligent. She is astounded that she is not the president of the company, and doesn't hesitate to let you know it.

Francis's non-stop chatter drives her co-workers crazy. She's always prattling on about the latest hot news, no matter how top secret it is. She is helpful and competent, but also nervous and insecure, and her secret stories give her a false sense of intimacy with her co-workers. In constant need of attention, she thrives on their laughter at her off-color jokes and their shock at the abundance and breadth of her inside scoops. She dares to use four-letter words, and tells risqué stories as part of her attention-seeking tactics. Francis is lonely, and she gossips so that she can be a part of the "in" crowd, which she never was and probably never will be. More than anything, she wants to be liked and included. Instead, she gets what she most fears: rejection and ridicule.

Francis came from an average middle-class family, and grew up in a small town in the Pacific Northwest. Her father had an obscure illness which required rest and quiet. So much attention was lavished upon her father that Francis felt neglected.

By the time Francis reached high school, she sought attention at any cost. She wasn't popular, and so decided to form her own group and make it into a desirable clique. Francis was resourceful. She began to set up her little world in a way that would work for her. She never connected her behavior with how neglected she had felt as a child and how much attention she felt she needed. She dressed in the brightest colors, spoke in a loud voice, and used only the most flamboyant gestures.

After she was hired by a midsize company, Francis replayed puberty over and over again. Once again she was not part of the "in" crowd, and she formed her own group which she was determined to make the envy of all the other cliques. If you watched her from a distance you would naturally feel sympathy, but having to interact with her on a daily basis would move you to disgust. It was hard on her co-workers, and as a result she suffered rejection on a regular basis.

The Chronic Cynic eagerly responds with "It can't happen," "It's not possible," or "There's no way" to almost any request. She will discuss her limitations as well as everyone else's. She is adamant that things simply will not work out, and treats the possibility of a happy ending with distaste and mild contempt.

Rita is a secretary. She calls herself assistant to the president, and at times personnel director, but she is really a secretary. She has been a secretary for twenty-five years. It's not that she likes her job, but rather that she cannot imagine doing anything else. She veers away from responsibility, yet likes to have control over her projects. She is prompt to arrive and prompt to leave. If you look for her thirty seconds after five, she's on the elevator. The only time there is light in her eyes is when she is talking about astrology. Doing people's charts is her passion, but she shies away from the thought of doing it to earn a living. Anything she truly wants is really not possible, and anything that you want is probably not possible either.

Rita went to a convent school where she was repeatedly told that she should take things on faith. If it was meant to be, God would make it happen. All power was in God's hands. Whenever she wanted anything, her father said, "Now, you know that if God wants it to happen, it will." She grew up denying any wants she had, and trusting that God would provide and decide. Whatever happened in her life was God's will, and she was obedient to it. Her seemingly cynical attitude was really a product of her religious training. In the workplace it translated into cynicism.

The Resigned Apathetic expresses his basic attitudes with such phrases as "It doesn't matter," "Nothing is ever going to change around here," and "Why bother?" He'll admit that his attitudes may change slightly for a short while, but they'll soon return to their original state. He is rarely enthusiastic or excited. His motto is "If it ain't broke, don't fix it!" He lives in a state of resignation and doesn't get aroused or upset about much. In fact, his reactions are always neutral. "It can't be done, if it hasn't been done before it isn't going to be done now, and you aren't going to make things any different, so don't even try."

These are the people who told the Wright brothers, "If man were meant to fly, God would have given him wings." They also said we'd never succeed in putting a man on the moon. If you have a new invention or idea, don't tell one of them, because they will only rain on your parade.

Gary is a downer unless you can maintain your sense of humor around him. Trying to describe him is like describing a bowl of oatmeal: it's tan, it's dense, and it's uninviting. Of medium height and build, with brown eyes and brown hair, he skulks unnoticed through the file room and turns up where you least expect him. People see Gary as a germ that may multiply, and they protect themselves instinctively from his negaholism.

Throughout his life, Gary was continually told "No" whenever he wanted anything. He was told he couldn't go to the college of his choice, that he couldn't marry the girl he wanted, and that he couldn't go into the career he desired. At a certain point in time, Gary got the message. He gave up. He was beaten. Dale, his father, told him that he set his sights too high and that he needed a dose of reality. Eventually Dale won, and Gary succumbed. It wasn't worth the fight.

Gary carried his defeat with him wherever he went.

He brought his defeat to the office, and his staff now experiences its own defeat. Gary spread his own brand of negaholism, and those who came in contact with him were contaminated.

SELF-SABOTAGE, OR SHOOTING YOURSELF IN THE FOOT

The four forms of negaholism—attitudinal, behavioral, mental, and verbal—represent all the various ways in which we sabotage ourselves and our corporation. Sabotage is the conscious or unconscious thought or action which impedes the progress of the corporation. Whenever a person engages in an activity which depreciates his own value, that of his co-workers, or of the corporation, he is displaying corporate negaholic behavior. This syndrome is usually deeply rooted and certainly widespread, but it is, in fact, curable. Frequently, people identify corporate life as a whole with these types of people and behaviors.

After reading about the different types of corporate negaholics, you probably identified either a boss, a subordinate, or, perhaps, even yourself! The next thing we need to do is determine how best to handle each situation.

CHAPTER 2

◆

HOW TO
DEAL WITH
A NEGAHOLIC
BOSS

If you have a negaholic boss, there are three things that you can do: you can quit and get another job; you can suffer and complain about the awful person for whom you have to work; or you can work with the situation so that you get what you want out of it. This last option is the most empowering and the most challenging. In order to get what you want from a negaholic boss, you first have to stop looking at your boss as the villain, and consequently to stop looking at yourself as the victim. You have to see yourself as capable and powerful enough to make a difference. You need to see this as a situation which affords you the opportunity to experiment and explore and see what works and what doesn't. You must believe that you can have a positive impact on the people in your environment. Before you approach the problem, you need to determine what kind of negaholic boss you have.

In Chapter One, I profiled fourteen different types of negaholics in the workplace. The ones who are most typically in managerial positions are: The Workaholic Workhorse, The Consummate Controller, The Political Peacemaker, and The Perennial Expert. From time to time, you will observe a Blatant Back-Stabber as well as a Status Quo Sustainer. You may also encounter six other negaholic boss types, which are: The Avoider and Denier, The Time Bomb, The Abusive Ogre, The Demotivating Dragon, The Overwhelming Avalanche, and The Spineless Sap.

THE AVOIDER AND DENIER

The avoider and denier manager could be interested in maintaining the status quo, or instead could be a person with blinders on who is just unable to confront the truth of a situation.

Mac is the head of the rehabilitation department in a midsize insurance company. He hasn't had a conversation with his direct subordinate, Brenda, in over a year, and both of them simply do their jobs. They don't address their breakdown in communications, nor do they even acknowledge that there is a problem. Mac goes to lunch every day and comes back smelling of alcohol. His employees smell the alcohol, mutter among themselves, and put up with an untenable situation. Most afternoons, Mac's reflexes are slower and everyone knows why. The scent on his breath is a direct tip-off. His staff members are torn between their loyalty to their boss, their fear of speaking up and losing their jobs, and the unpleasant option of putting up with working for someone whom they don't respect and with whom they can't communicate. The situation has been like this for so long that people accept it as normal.

In a conversation with me, Brenda, Mac's direct subordinate, admitted that there was a problem. She was confused about the situation and didn't know what to do about it. She described her disgust at seeing a bright and capable man deteriorate before her very eyes. She commented on how people didn't know whether to bypass their boss entirely or go to him and accept his directives. People were confused about the leadership of the department, primarily because his decision-making ability was hampered and his behavior was inconsistent. Since Brenda spoke with a tremble in her voice, it was clear that she was fearful of even addressing the situation. She didn't want to get anybody in trouble. She didn't want to be the one to blow the whistle. She was nervous and uneasy telling the staff's secret to an outsider. Several times in our conversation, she brought up her fear of doing the wrong thing. It was only with a great deal of reassurance that she was willing to discuss the situation and consider confronting both her fear of speaking up and the prospect of doing something about her boss.

After our discussion, I thought about the best way to approach this delicate issue. It had to be dealt with in a very discreet manner. No one should be indicted, yet at the same time the problem needed to be addressed. The situation was clearly dysfunctional, since this was a taboo topic kept secret by all co-dependents and avoided at all costs. With no intervention, it would continue indefinitely.

An intervention is a meeting where people who care enough to tell the truth confront a person who is denying his or her condition. The desired outcome is for the communication of the truth to shift the situation from dysfunctional to functional. Although intervention is usually specifically related to substance abuse, it needn't be. Interventions are never comfortable and can be highly confrontational, but they are often essential if a problem is going to be remedied. Interventions are one of the only sure ways to deal with denial and avoidance.

The first thing I did was to ask Brenda's permission to talk about this situation with the president of the company. I then had a conversation with him in which I discussed the need for confidentiality and a strategy which would take into consideration all those involved and their individual needs. The president agreed that an intervention was in order. The next step was to ask Brenda if she would be willing to take part in it. At first she was dead set against it, but after considering her prospects for the future, she gradually became willing to take a risk and face her fear.

I called a meeting with Brenda and Mac. The purpose of the meeting, I said, was to facilitate their communication as work associates, since I understood that they hadn't talked in over a year. I asked Brenda to describe to Mac her experience of working with him. She was fearful, and would have preferred to be anywhere in the world rather than in this meeting. With some coaxing, she told him how bright and valuable he was to the company and specifically to her department, and how, because of his alcohol consumption at lunch, she and others had lost respect for him. She said that she didn't want to get him into trouble, but just wanted to clear things up so that they could work together again. She also said how afraid she had been of this meeting. He started out defensively, but with encouragement opened up to what she was saying as well as to her inner turmoil. His response was profound. He was determined to do something about his situation. With the authorization I had received from the president, I offered the assistance of the company in dealing with his situation. He was appreciative, and I let him know that I was there as a safe haven to support him in this difficult time. Mac thanked Brenda for having the guts to do what no one else had had the courage to do previously.

In a private conversation with Brenda after the intervention, she said that she couldn't believe that she had lived through the meeting. She said it had been one of the toughest things she had ever done. She had been mortally afraid of telling the truth but had gone ahead and done it anyway. She faced her fear and had been victorious. She had a whole new sense of self-respect because of the courage she found in herself. She felt as if she had done something that she was incapable of doing, and she felt bigger and stronger as a result of the meeting. Not only had she found respect for Mac, but she had found self-respect as well.

Mac went through an alcohol detoxification program and returned to his job a stronger person, more available to his employees, and better able to cope with his job. It was a breakthrough for Brenda, Mac, and the company. All involved won by confronting their dysfunctions.

THE TIME BOMB

The Time Bomb is the boss who is inconsistent. One minute he is sweet, kind, and considerate, and the next minute he is talking to you as if you were a complete moron. His moods are hard to predict. He is fun and supportive, and then all of a sudden he snaps, as if for no reason at all, and becomes deprecating. You don't want to upset him, so you tiptoe around him as though he were a land-mine.

Jason was a highly competent assistant to the CEO of a large title company. Because of his ability to produce results, he was the ideal person to be number two in command. He had a high need for autonomy and, left to his own devices, could be counted on to get almost any job done. Jason was talking to Sandy about her project. She started complaining about the lack of information that she had and told him how difficult it was to gather any information given the lack of parameters. All of a sudden, he turned on her and said, "All you do is whine. I'm sick of you complaining all the time. Why don't you grow up and act your age!" Sandy, on the verge of tears, was shocked and startled to hear him lash out at her. She wasn't at all prepared for his reaction. She held back the tears and fled from his office. He turned to me and said, "Emotional females. You can't tell them anything without them overreacting."

Jason needed to be right. You could detect it in his conversations. Jason was right, and everyone else was always wrong. It was Sam's fault, or Jack did it, or it was that idiot Ted. You never heard Jason say, "I really blew it," or "I need to learn how to manage women better." He was convinced that he was right and the rest of the world was wrong. I tried various tactics with him, but I couldn't make a dent.

Finally I saw an opening. The key to Jason's situation was timing. I had to wait for the right moment, for something to happen to him which affected him deeply enough to render him just slightly vulnerable. The situation which finally afforded me this opportunity involved his nine-year-old daughter. His ex-wife had threatened to withhold visitation rights, and he was shaken to the core. I asked him if we could talk. He agreed. When I asked him what was going on, he said, "I don't know what I would do if I couldn't see her. She means everything to me. I have to figure out a way to get a hold of her so that Lila can't threaten me like that."

I asked if he were talking about his ex-wife or his child. He said that his ex-wife had made him really angry by threatening him, and that he wanted to see his daughter whenever he wanted. I asked if he would give me a little leeway with him.

"Sure," he said.

"You can blame your ex-wife, that's the easy way, but maybe, just maybe, there are some lessons to be learned here which could be valuable."

"Like what?" he said belligerently.

"If you're going to talk to me like that, I'm not going to say anything. But if you're willing to listen, then maybe you can learn something new."

"O.K." he said. "But she's never been right about anything."

"Maybe not, but if you always have to be right about everything, it's awfully hard for anyone else to teach you anything at all."

He shook his head and said he was willing to listen. I reminded him that he didn't have to listen to me, but that this was about his child. He seemed about as open as I had ever seen him, and so I took the opportunity to say some things which otherwise I never would have dared.

"Jason, have you ever noticed how often Mike, Ted, Bob, and Sandy are wrong?"

"No, I guess I haven't," he said.

"Either you're working with the biggest group of baboons in the world, or else you only focus on what they do wrong, and ignore what they do right." He looked at me quizzically. "You see, managing people is a process of learning what works with each person individually. Each person is different, and what works with one doesn't necessarily work with another. The challenge is finding out what works with each one, and then doing it. If you end up making them wrong, judging them, finding fault, and calling them names, then you aren't ever going to learn something new. You'll just end up being right."

He thought for a minute, then said, "But what does that have to do with my little Jenny?"

"It sounds like the same thing is happening with your ex-wife. Unless you find out what is really going *on* in this situation versus what is going to *work*, you won't have the chance to learn anything new. You'll just be committed to being right and getting even."

He thought and then said, "You mean there's a parallel between my home life and my job?"

"Usually we like to keep them separate, but the truth is that we are the same person in each situation, and chances are that we use the same problem-solving skills at home and in the office."

"So what are you suggesting?" he asked defensively.

"I'm not suggesting anything," I said, "but if you want to learn something, you might try a new tack. Instead of just writing people off, see if there isn't something to learn from what they are saying. Ask yourself if you have to be right every time, or if it would be more helpful to see someone else's point of view for a change."

He thought and thought. Finally he said, "I love

that little girl. I don't want to lose her. Can you help me keep her?"

"Maybe," I said, "but it will require a behavior change from you. The old ways don't work anymore, and you have to let go of them, or I won't waste my time trying to help."

He looked skeptical but a tiny bit hopeful. "You mean you would be willing to help me?"

"Perhaps, but you need to listen to me and really seriously consider what I am saying, then talk to me about your reactions instead of just writing me off like you do everyone else."

He said he was willing, and so I became his personal management coach. He was difficult. When he became intolerably arrogant or obstinate, I would refuse to work with him. He would ultimately soften, come around, and ask why I had withdrawn. When he asked, I would always inquire whether he really wanted to know, and if he said "yes," I would tell him. His progress was slow and time-consuming, but gradually he grew and changed. He became capable of admitting his mistakes; he stopped judging the world and started looking at what his own role in it was. I grew to really care about Jason, and so did the people he worked with.

THE ABUSIVE OGRE

Hal completed the marketing plan. It was done on time. He did what he was asked to do. And then he was told:

"The marketing plan has only three main facets when it should have at least twelve. I told you to expand on the ideas we tossed around, not just restate them. The way the page is lined up is all wrong—the margins are too narrow. When this is bound you won't be able to read the print. There's a typo on page two, fourth paragraph down, line five. You didn't include any graphics. I told you we needed pictures. Where are the pictures? It's unacceptable."

Once again, Hal had done his job only to be devastated by the response to it. It seemed that no matter what he did, Robert would find something wrong with his work. Hal could pour his heart and soul into a project, and Robert would find a typo or a lack of continuity. If it was a really sound proposal, he might just throw the whole thing out on principle. Robert never mentioned that the project actually was done and done on time; all he did was harp on what was wrong, and in such a way that Hal couldn't learn much from his mistakes. Robert always noticed what was wrong, never what was right. He managed others much the same way his father did. He felt it built character to point out someone's weaknesses. Sometimes he would even "develop" the character of his individual staff members in front of customers or peers. It was humiliating to have him invalidate you in front of other people. Violating the number one rule of good management (Never mete out correction or discipline in front of others) was his rule of thumb.

Cynical and unhappy, but a highly intelligent manager, infinitely capable of doing his job, Robert had no idea how severely he damaged Hal's and others' self-esteem. He believed that "no idea is a good idea," and he seized every opportunity to prove it. Robert was part of the corporate "in" crowd that decided who made the grade and who didn't. If John, the VP, liked you, then Robert, his direct subordinate, liked you; it was as simple as that. If you didn't measure up in John's book, then Robert would make sure that you were out of the club. Robert was also very political and would always side with the strongest team.

Things started out well for Hal. Robert provided input and guidance. At a certain point, though, John, the VP, decided that Hal was unacceptable. After four months, when the company merged with another airline, things started to change. Hal was given the responsibility to make the merger work. However, he was not given the authority to execute the task. Disorganization reigned. There seemed to be no master plan, no coordination of efforts between the different groups, and no communication about tasks and priorities. Hal was the designated referee without a jersey, so all the players simply ignored and bypassed him. His job was overwhelming, and he didn't see a way that he could win. For example, the catering company which supplied passenger meals on flights didn't know how many passengers would be on board any specific flight, and thus didn't know how many meals to put on the planes.

Everything Hal requested was denied. Every idea he proposed was rejected. Every plan, solution, or strategy was unequivocally disregarded. He felt demoralized and deflated. He requested support in terms of marketing, money, and schedule adjustments. He proposed a new seating arrangement in the gate area, more training to improve the quality of service, and direct-mail campaigns. No matter what he proposed, the answer was always "No." He finally came up with a plan to allocate advertising money based upon market size and revenue potential, taking into consideration the media. Hal entitled the formula "brand development index," and he submitted a preliminary plan to Robert and then to

John. Upon first perusal, they both said it seemed viable and agreed to back it. Hal was delighted with their reaction and set out to design a proposal which would fulfill all of their needs and wishes.

After a week, Hal approached Robert and eagerly asked about his response to the proposal. Robert turned to Hal, who was brimming with happy anticipation, and said, "Oh that, I threw it away." Hal was visibly shaken, but mustered up the courage to inquire why. Robert replied, "It's a marketing plan for our competitor, not us. We could never allocate advertising dollars that way. Those suggestions are far too sophisticated for us—we're never going to do anything like that. It's obvious that you simply don't understand our culture. It's hard for me to believe that you've been with us for eight months and still don't understand the way we do business. If you want to do something like that, go work for our competitor. It will never happen with us."

Hal was devastated. His enthusiasm for the project and for his job evaporated completely. He didn't give up, though. A new opportunity came along which seemed to have promise. A board game was being designed in which commercial companies would have the opportunity to have their name printed on one of the spaces on the board and at the same time allocate discount coupons to game players. Hal thought this was a very creative idea, and was interested in both the exposure and the potential business that could be generated through the coupon allocation. The cost of a space on the board was $30,000, and the discount coupon was going to be $50 off the cost of a ticket on their airline. Hal put together a proposal, including all the pros and cons, the costs, and the projected revenues. His proposal was not only rejected, it was ridiculed. The dis-

47

count was reduced from $50 to $10. The suggestion of participating in a board game was mocked and became an office joke. Hal was once again demoralized.

Hal was then told to increase his airline's business-traveler market share. He proposed added-value programs, direct-mail programs which offered discounts to professional associations in specific areas, a merchandise-based frequent-flyer program, advertising full-price coach fares which would be confirmed in first class if a seat were available, and frequent-flyer programs which were tied into rental cars and hotels. Every idea that he came up with was shot down. Every time he tried to do his job, he found himself thwarted. Both Robert and John tried to convince Hal in insidious ways that he could do nothing right, that he wasn't capable or intelligent, and that his ideas were worthless.

Robert didn't want to discuss anything personal; his total focus was on the airline business. He liked to ridicule almost anything: people, situations, politics, minority groups, even religion. His comments were bigoted, and he would make disparaging jokes and asides about individuals and groups. He enjoyed times when people were combative and nasty. He exhibited a fiendish delight when the tenor of the conversation became biting and vicious.

Hal and Robert had many friends in common, and there was a subtle competition between them regarding everything, including their social lives. Hal was always interested in Robert's background and what influences had made him the way he was. When he inquired he found out little, except for the fact that Robert's mother had died young and that he had had a difficult childhood. Robert's relationship with his father was strained, he had felt out of place in school, and he had few friends. He was, however, very intelligent, even though he grew bitter and cynical. He had a chip on his shoulder, and it was tough for Hal to figure out why. Robert had never been very happy in any job that he had. He wanted authority and responsibility but shirked all the blame.

Hal had been and still was a good boy who would always put his best foot forward but often feel misunderstood, unappreciated, and thwarted. It had started in childhood, in his relationship with his father, and continued on through adulthood. More than anything he wanted to be respected, appreciated, and recognized, but what he received instead was always the antithesis of that.

When I asked Hal why the office culture promoted such abusive behaviors, he said, "The people at the top are not customer-driven or employee-driven. The airline is completely price-driven, with no particular focus on the customer. It believes that there are enough other people out there who will fly with us because of our low fares, so it doesn't have to worry about alienating customers because there will always be more. Employees do not come to this airline for a career, but rather for a job. The current president vacillates between heavy involvement and no involvement at all." It seemed no wonder that this major airline kept bouncing in and out of bankruptcy. It is still around today, heaping abuse on anyone who is willing to tolerate it, ignoring customers, and perpetuating its negaholic culture.

THE DEMOTIVATING DRAGON

Don was the director of operations for a property management company. He had a winning smile whenever he chose to rise above his perennial suspicious look. His way of saying "good job" was to say "Not bad." He never said, "Wow, you did a great job. You were terrific." His response to the comment, "Isn't it a beautiful day?" was "It could be worse." When Don visited a property, the general mood always started out well. Later, after he had completed reviewing each department and had pointed out all the bad news, the entire staff was crestfallen. Morale took a nosedive every time Don did the Negaholic Rag. All the good news was taken for granted, and all the bad news was highlighted and broadcast all over town. After he left, his staff had the feeling that it couldn't do anything right and probably never would.

There are ways to deal with a person like Don, and the first rule is to keep your sense of humor. Give him a blank list numbered from one to ten, and tell him that before he leaves he must fill it in with good news. Mail him a piece of paper which says, "I want to thank you, my wonderful staff, for the following:" On an attached memo, stipulate that by the time he arrives he needs to have it completed with a minimum of five (or ten) items. Formulate rules for Don, such as that for every area that needs corrective action, he must find another area which deserves applause. Start an employee of the month club, and create mini-ceremonies celebrating the employee with the most sales, or the most customer commendations, or the most votes in the appreciation box. In other words, make a game out of turning him into the kind of manager you want.

THE OVERWHELMING AVALANCHE

Julie was a project factory. She was a visionary who saw a million possibilities and deeply wanted to make a difference. An undaunted mass of creative energy who seemed to be active twenty-four hours a day, she could think up more good ideas than anyone, and then pass them on to Miriam, her assistant. Miriam was devoted to Julie, and would do anything to support her in the realization of her visions. Miriam's respect and admiration for Julie got in the way of her taking care of her own personal needs. Miriam's absences started to increase: first it was an afternoon, then a full day, then a day here, a day there, and then her presence became very unpredictable.

Julie called me in to work on the problem. "I just never know when she'll be here," said Julie. "She's been out so frequently lately that I don't know if I can depend on her anymore."

I asked if I could meet with each of them separately and with both of them together. Julie agreed enthusiastically. "Anything you can do to help us out would be wonderful. I just want to support Miriam in being healthy, happy, and productive."

When I met with Miriam, it was evident that she had set no boundaries with Julie, was unable to say "No," and was buried under the avalanche of Julie's projects. The "To Do's" had gotten to her, and she was now sick and unable to do any of them. She felt physically and emotionally depleted, and guilty for not being in the office.

"I just can't do it all," she said to me. "As soon as I start to tackle a project, she gives me five others. I never seem to get dug out from any of them, and now it's hopeless."

I asked her how she felt inside.

"Like I'm a failure," she said. "I just can't win at this. I can never get ahead. There is no use in trying."

"What would you need to succeed?" I asked with interest.

"I would need to be able to complete something. I would need to see the fruits of my labors and feel the satisfaction of seeing a project through," she said dolefully.

After I met with Julie and Miriam separately, I met with them together. When we met, I encouraged them both to talk about what they needed to succeed, what would bring them satisfaction, and how to tell each other if either were unhappy.

Julie wanted Miriam to be "in the open," and available to receive the next ball that was being passed. Julie didn't care if Miriam then passed the ball to someone else or put it in the basket herself. In other words, Julie was willing for Miriam to hire other staff if necessary, to oversee the tasks, have them executed, and be available to receive the next job. Julie saw Miriam as an executive administrative assistant who should orchestrate projects and not necessarily work on them. Miriam, on the other hand, saw herself as "the doer" who had to handle everything herself. Miriam felt that she had to have hands-on contact with everything that came across her desk. When Julie would say "I want you to know everything. I want you to be fully informed about all of my affairs," Miriam would interpret that to mean, "You are responsible, I want you to personally do every task I give you."

As our meetings progressed, it became apparent that Miriam had to start speaking up. She needed to restate what she had heard so that she could get confirmation and not operate from assumptions. She needed to say when she had more on her plate than she could conceivably handle. Miriam needed to manage Julie, her boss, and take charge of the situation because Julie was a limitless fountain of creativity. She needed to propose plans to handle the plethora of projects so that she didn't get snowed under, and end up sick. She also needed to have a cadre of extra temporary support people who, like firefighters, could come in to handle the emergencies and then go away.

Julie had to observe more closely Miriam's condition, reactions, and general demeanor. She had to tune in to the relationship between the two of them and not just focus on tasks. Julie had to realize that Miriam was a real, live person who needed caretaking and attention like anyone else. She needed to take a deep breath and remember that the reason Miriam was there was because of the relationship between them, not just because of the tasks or the job.

They both had lessons to learn, but as things go, the patterns left over from each of their childhoods matched remarkably. Julie was rewarded for her creativity and task management, and Miriam was recognized for her attention to details. Miriam would never admit that she couldn't get it all done and would sooner die than shout "Uncle!" They agreed to communicate before there was an emergency, to support each other in winning, and to work together in brainstorming solutions to problems rather than isolating themselves and muscling it through.

THE SPINELESS SAP

Ralph sat at his desk shuffling papers. He wondered why none of his staff came and met with him. He told them time and time again that his door was always open and that they could come to him with any problem. After repeated attempts, his employees soon discovered that Ralph was spineless when it came to making a difference in the organization. Whether the issues had to do with confusion about direction, personnel conflicts, requests for materials, manpower, or recommendations, the answer was always a ponderous, "Let me think about that. I'll get back to you," and then nothing would happen. The issue would fade away as if the discussion had never happened. He wouldn't follow up, get back to them, or give a definite answer, and the requests just disappeared into space.

Suzie asked for a rubber stamp to mark "Paid" on an invoice. The expense was probably not more than $2.50 at a stationery store. After she requested the same item three times, she was frustrated and finally went out and spent her own money on it. Tracy requested a refrigerator in which to store the employee lunches. The answer wasn't "Yes" or "No," it was simply nonexistent. She finally went over Ralph's head to ask his boss how they could have a refrigerator purchased and installed. The job got done without Ralph.

At Christmas time the company was swamped with mail, and several of the employees suggested that a temporary employee could help with opening the mail and forwarding it to the right department. Again, the Spineless Sap, Ralph, would act concerned, promise to "Get back," and then do nothing. The employees banded together and got the requisition approved, but again it was in spite of Ralph.

If you have a Spineless Sap as a boss, realize that whatever you do nothing will happen. Out of respect for his position, keep him informed about what you plan to do, then go ahead and take action. Always send his boss your memos and tell him about your actions so that all people are fully informed about your motives, plans, and doings. If you sit and wait, behaving yourself, you will be frustrated. With this type of person it is better to ask for forgiveness than to ask for permission. The main motto is go ahead and do it anyway, and if you make a mess, clean it up later.

BATTLING BOSSES IN THE NEGA-TRENCHES

It does no good to battle your boss. If you find that you are having difficulties with your boss, there are three options: figure out the best way to work around him, sit down and communicate, or leave the job. Complaining and colluding do not help your situation, your boss's ability to get his job done, or the department you work in.

If you are going to communicate, you need to determine what you want to say. Avoid accusations, name-calling, and criticism. Use sentences that start with "I" or "It seems to me." Avoid generalizing and universalizing behavior. Stay away from the words "always" and "never," which bring out the defensiveness in people and invite an argument. When you approach your boss, treat any communication problems as if they are yours; don't blame them on him. Let him know that you want to build a healthy work relationship, and that you are searching for the best way for the two of you to work together. Remember, sometimes you have to manage your boss in managing you. Not all managers have been trained in how to manage, nor do they always remember what they have learned. If you take the initiative, but do it supportively, you'll be amazed at the results.

The second option is to work around your boss. If sitting down and communicating is too confrontational, then ask others who have worked with him for a long period what their strategy is. Interview them to find out what works, and then just do it.

If the first two options are unsatisfactory, then request a transfer to another department or pull out your résumé. The last option is to stay where you are and do nothing, but that would just reinforce your negaholism.

If you want to know how to manage the negaholic employee, the next chapter has lots of hot tips for you.

CHAPTER 3

◆

HOW TO MANAGE YOUR NEGAHOLIC EMPLOYEE

If you have a negaholic employee, you can either transfer him to another department, terminate him, or invest time, money, and effort to develop him into a healthy, productive, and useful member of your office team.

Managing a negaholic employee means spending a lot of time trying to motivate him and avoiding upsetting him, which would create a bigger problem than you already have. Some negaholic employees are very challenging because they may be highly competent but have a low self-image, which requires some skill in handling. Then there are others who have all the appearances and features of being great employees, but something isn't right and you just can't figure out what. Still others occupy a great deal of your time and attention, because although they do support work for you, you spend a lot of your time supporting them.

From the list of fourteen types of negaholics in Chapter One, there are certain types who naturally fall into the negaholic employee category. Some of them are: The Rebellious Rabble-Rouser, The Solitary Succeeder, The Erratic Eccentric, The Morose Melancholic, The Walking Wounded, The Garrulous Gossip, The Chronic Cynic, and The Resigned Apathetic. There are six additional types of negaholic employees. They are: The Pathetic Pouter, The Arrogant Argonaut, The Depressed and Diminished, The Abused and Beaten, The Resistant Recalcitrant, and the Radiant Robot. These six are in a class of their own. They are the extreme cases who are more difficult to deal with than the normal fourteen negaholic prototypes. I will describe these six additional types even though they are extreme, since they do appear in the workplace from time to time and you must know how to deal with them.

THE PATHETIC POUTER

Estelle mopes around the office with a hangdog expression on her face. She approaches tasks with reticence and nervousness. She has a batting average of .333, in that projects have to be redone three times to get them right. She knows how to do the job, but she has such a fear of making mistakes that she bungles the most rudimentary tasks. She is intelligent, but she is so insecure that she psyches herself out of tasks which she already knows perfectly well how to do.

The annual report was being assembled for review before being sent to the printer. Different employees were pulling together the pieces of the document and putting them into a binder, with tabs dividing the various sections. Estelle was frantically racing around the office in a tizzy. She couldn't get the sections straight. She kept getting confused. She was told several times that the report of the board of management came before the financial information, and that all the supplemental information came at the end. She kept asking the same question over and over again, until finally one of the team wrote out the order on a piece of paper so that she could refer back to it and follow it whenever she needed.

Estelle asks questions that she already knows the answers to. I would call them "dumb" questions, but I like to think there are no such things. After the fifth call from the insurance person came in, she would ask, "Do we have Steve's number around the office?" It wouldn't occur to her to take down the number when Steve called in and enter it on the Rolodex. Instead, she comes to her boss and asks for the number three times. She would say, after working in the office for two years, "How do I order photocopying paper?" When she types a letter, she doesn't automatically make a correction or look up a word in the dictionary. When asked why she didn't correct a typo, she would say, "I thought you had a reason for typing it that way." As her manager you would want to scream at her, sit her down, and find out if she had a serious problem, or tear your hair out in frustration.

The best way to handle someone like Estelle is not in the heat of the moment, but rather when you have calmed down and no longer want to strangle her. Do not explode. Instead, document each instance which drove you crazy. Write down the subject, the place, the time, and as much of the conversation as you can remember. Then write down the questions you had about the interaction. For instance: "Can you tell me what you were thinking when you said that?" Or: "I know you know the answer, so why did you ask me that question?" Or: "Tell me what goes on with you when you forget things that you know how to do. Like for instance when . . ." Let her know that you are eager to understand what makes her tick, and that it is safe for her to speak openly. It is important to let her know that you are on her side and want to support her, and that you are interested in finding out the best way to do that.

When I worked with Estelle, I had to help her get beyond her terror of making mistakes. I had to encourage her to tell me what she was feeling rather than giving me an inane comment off the top of her head. If she confessed to me that she was scared of making a mistake, then we could deal with that. If she said she thought I just wanted the words misspelled, it would incur my wrath, which would only compound the situation. Taking the time to talk to an employee is an investment in that person's growth. If you deem the person worth it, then investing in her is what you need to do. It takes time, energy, and care to grow a great employee.

THE ARROGANT ARGONAUT

Mandy, Vera's boss, was having a problem with her. Though Mandy couldn't pinpoint it, Vera's problem seemed to be affecting all the other employees as well. Mandy asked us to conduct a seminar on team-building, which we proceeded to do.

We assembled all of the employees in a room early

one morning. As we stood in the seminar room, no one spoke. We asked simple questions: What is a team? When have you been a part of a team? Do you have a team here, on the job? No one said a word. It was strange. We had never run into this type of situation before. Even if people are timid or reticent, there is always someone who will break the ice. There is always one talker in each group. These people were scared to talk, and we didn't know why. We encouraged them to say something, even to address why they weren't talking. All were silent.

The seminars we conduct are participatory. We ask questions, and the participants are supposed to come up with answers to open-ended questions which then stimulate the discussion. When they volunteer solutions to their problems, they are more motivated to implement them. Our style is experiential, the method is socratic, and the mode is participative. We usually don't lecture and tell people what to do or how to be. The lecture part comes after all of their thoughts, ideas, and comments have been volunteered.

On this occasion, we trainers looked at each other and decided that we had to go against all of our beliefs and spend a few minutes lecturing. We closed the seminar fairly early and conducted individual meetings with the participants to find out what was going on and why they wouldn't speak. After they were promised confidentiality, they ventured out and timidly described what it was like to work in that environment. Their loyalty to their boss and co-workers, their fear of being labeled "insubordinate," and their terror of retaliation kept them mute. There was a moment when one brave person broke the ice.

Bart said, "If we tell you the truth, we will be punished so severely that it isn't worth the price. You don't know how bad it can get. And besides, you can come in here, stir things up, and then leave, but we have to stay here and live with the aftermath. You consultants are all alike. You're just one more consultant who is going to come in here, make a big flurry, promise to make things better, and when you leave it's worse than if you never came."

"It sounds like you've had some bad experiences, both on the job as well as with other consultants," I said. "Can you tell me about some of those experiences?"

"What's the use? It won't do any good. Besides, you'll just put it in your report, some big shot will file it in a drawer, and nothing will ever come of it."

"Maybe you're right. Maybe this *is* an exercise in wasting time. But for my own sanity, would you tell me what's going on? O.K., let's say that we go away and everything stays the same as it was, are you any better off? You're in the same place you were before. So what so awful can happen to you if you let me in on what's happening?"

"Obviously you don't know how mean she can be. She takes revenge on us and we'll all suffer if we say anything," Bart said with foreboding.

"Who?" I inquired, sounding a bit like an owl. "Who is going to punish you?"

"I can't tell you. Then you'll know, and it'll be awful," he said with conviction.

"Hey, you get to live with this fear for the rest of your work life, or at least until you leave this job. I guess you want it this way."

"Listen, I'm getting out of here as soon as I get my transfer," he said.

"Great, so since you're leaving, what's the story? Why won't people talk? Come on, you've got nothing to lose!"

"It's Vera, our manager. She's vindictive. She rules this place with an iron hand, and if we do anything that she doesn't like, she takes it out on us by docking our pay, taking away our sick days, and denying us the days off we request. She also writes us up and puts it in our file. She humiliates us in front of the customers, and she makes fools of us. It's just awful. She's mean, and I can't wait to get out of here."

"Thanks for telling me. Now, what can we do about the situation? If we're going to make any changes happen, you need to help us," I said matter-of-factly.

"We need to have a meeting without her present, and then the employees will talk," Bart replied with certainty.

"As a consultant, one of my capital rules is to have management present at all meetings. If we're to go against that rule, it means that we're taking as big a risk as you are by talking to me now. I'm willing to risk it, but we're in this together. I'll talk to Vera and tell her that there has been a request that we meet without her present, and see her response. If she agrees, we'll do it."

I asked Vera if she would honor a request by the staff to meet with us without her. She said she didn't care, and if that's what they wanted, so be it. It was with great trepidation that we met in a private meeting room without Vera. I felt like we were committing a crime by setting up an environment to deliberately talk about Vera behind her back, but at that point it seemed like the best alternative.

In the meeting, Bart told the staff that he had already told us the worst of it, that he had requested the meeting without Vera, and that it was O.K. to talk. He urged them to speak their minds, and really pushed them until they finally started to describe how afraid they were to say anything. One by one they began to open up. Tales of fear, demoralization, hurt, and repression were abundant. Several even started to cry, mostly from relief at finally telling the truth about Vera. It was extraordinary to see the deep level of hurt that could occur in a work environment. After they had told their stories of mental, interpersonal, and in some cases physical abuse, they felt better. But the question still remained, what were we going to do about it? I asked them what were they willing to risk to have their environment transformed. I told them that I wasn't sure what would work, or exactly what we could do, but that I was committed to try whatever they believed would help.

They wanted me to ask Vera to come into the room, have Bart act as spokesperson for the employees, and see how she responded to their concerns. Again, I was nervous. First they wanted to meet together without her, then they wanted to bring her in and communicate their deepest hurts and resentments. I met with Vera privately and told her what the employees had requested. I gave her a choice, and said that if she didn't want to meet with them in a group, she didn't have to. I let her know that she could meet with them one by one, if they were willing, or later, at a better time for her. Then I said firmly, "But if you come into the room and listen to their concerns, you must not defend, argue, or justify your actions. You need to simply be open and listen, and if you can't do that, then I don't want you to come into the meeting room." She thought about it for a moment, and said that she wasn't afraid and was very curious to hear what they had to say.

Vera came into the meeting room with me, and what transpired was truly remarkable. I worked as a co-trainer with my partner, who coached the employees on how to communicate their feelings. While I had been meeting with Vera privately, she had been laying the ground rules with the employees. They were urged to describe specific situations and how they had felt during their interaction with Vera. They were to refrain from attacking, accusing, name-calling, blaming, or from making any disparaging comments. Meanwhile I worked with Vera, coaching her to listen and to hear what they had to say. We all lived through the meeting, although there were moments when I thought we wouldn't. Privately, I told Vera that after the meeting there could be no hint of threats, retaliation, or negative consequences for any of those present.

THE BOSS AS EMPLOYEE

I met with Vera and her boss, Mandy. Mandy, who was very fond of Vera, could not believe her ears. She was shocked that Vera's employees had such severe problems with her. Clearly, Mandy had been in denial and ignored the clues which had come to her in many different forms. We all talked about the situation and started to review the options. One option was to terminate Vera. The second option was a transfer. The third option was to deal with the situation head-on, and re-habilitate, train, and develop Vera as a healthy manager. All of the alternatives were put on the table, and

Mandy and Vera both opted for the most difficult choice of all, transformation.

We had to outline a strategy which would take into consideration all possible situations: interviewing, hiring, orienting new employees, running meetings, handling discipline issues, giving correction, scheduling shifts and days off—but most important, one-on-one meetings between Vera and her staff. Lynn (my partner), Mandy, and I put together a plan to coach Vera to be present for these important moments, monitor her behavior, and give her meaningful feedback. At first Vera was split in two: the part that wanted to grow and the part that thought she knew it all. She would start out willingly enough, but then become defensive and resistant. Each time we would have to remind her of her stated objectives. She would remember why we were there, give us permission to critique her, what she had said, or how she had said it, and then we could make some progress. She needed to learn how her attitude, tone of voice, gestures, body language, and abruptness affected other people. She had no understanding of how others could be devastated by the flash of her eyes or the abrupt tone of her voice.

Vera's individual coaching was long and slow, and at times seemed like a complete waste of energy. After two years of individual attention and improvement through steady increments, it happened. Vera's store was suddenly the top-producing store in all of the northern region. Her employees attributed it to her management style. We were all flabbergasted. We had been so close to the forest that we had lost sight of the trees. The magic had happened. We believed in the process, but when it actually happened, we could barely believe the results. An impossible dream had once again come true.

This kind of result only happens with a manager who is committed to seeing the process through, coupled with an employee who is willing, at least most of the time, to improve.

THE DEPRESSED AND DIMINISHED

Penny had a sweet demeanor and a ready smile that gave you the feeling she didn't have an unkind thought in her head. Her cheery façade and pleasant tone, however, camouflaged a deep-seated belief that things just don't work out, no matter how hard you try. She always reacted in a way that reinforced her pessimistic convictions.

Penny's negaholism was evident when you presented positive solutions to her perplexing relationships with her two stepsons. It seeped out when she would talk about her dream vacation, and then say it was only a dream and would never happen. Even when she would get exactly what she wanted, she would undercut herself by saying, "Yeah, but it was time you got a computer anyway," or, "Oh, that was just luck." She requested a work table, a bulletin board, a computer, her own desk; when she received them, she was appreciative but gave herself no credit. She didn't associate her request with an item's appearance. She had trouble celebrating her accomplishments and victories, and found it much easier to be forlorn and depressed.

If someone at work came up with an exciting proposal, she would comment, "They'll never go for that. They probably don't have any money in the budget. They're much too conservative!" Being around her drained your energy. Amazingly enough, she had no idea that she was a negaholic, but saw herself instead as a happy, well-adjusted, cheerful person. There was a clear discrepancy between the way she viewed herself and the way her associates saw her.

When asked how she was, Penny would always say "Fine," her sad tone suggesting that things were not "fine" at all. She would always put herself last and everyone else first. She cooked, cleaned, organized, babysat, ironed, cleaned up, and did everything for the family. She also held down two jobs on the side. Through it all, she never received the recognition she wanted and deserved. She was miserable, but she thought that being unhappy was her cross to bear as a woman.

To bring about change in your life, you must have the desire, the willingness, the belief, and the commitment to cause things to be different. It was very unsatisfying to work with Penny at first because she didn't have the belief that things could be different or the commitment to change them. You can't make the impossible happen unless everyone involved buys in to the vision. People need to be given choices and the opportunity to take charge of their own lives and make them different.

Finally, Penny turned around. She said, "I want things to be different and I want you to help me." I said, "We can go forward and take action if you are really on board." It had taken a lot of listening, hand-holding, encouragement, and pep talks, but she finally made the move for herself. She still has trouble putting herself first, but now at least she knows it's something to watch out for. She is more willing to focus on solutions rather than on problems, and on taking action rather than on giving up.

THE ABUSED AND BEATEN

Trish attracted trouble. She was pretty, with light-brown hair tied back in a ponytail, a peach-apricot complexion, and a compact, athletic body. She was very enthusiastic, with lots of energy, but she had one tragic flaw: she was constantly enmeshed in personal dramas.

At first glance you would think she was bright, capable, and a real go-getter; but she didn't believe in herself deep down, and she created daily calamities which prevented her from succeeding at her job. First, her phone was about to be disconnected because of a friend who ran up her phone bill while staying at her house. Then she was about to be evicted because she couldn't pay the rent. Following the rent debacle, she discovered that her boyfriend was on drugs. The next nightmare was that her sister was going to have a serious operation and she herself was too traumatized to function in the office. She came into work one Monday morning with tales of the night before, when she had witnessed a knife fight outside a bar. It was astounding how one individual could attract so many calamities.

The traumas and tragedies were a daily occurrence. Trish was so busy handling emergencies that she had little time to do her job. These disasters were supposed to explain her lateness, her absences, her phone calls on the job, her emotional condition on the job, and her general state of disorganization. Her attention was not on her job, not on her work, and not on any facet of the business except getting her paycheck.

After several conversations with Trish, during which I gave her some choices for the future, she chose personal drama and her present lifestyle over the job. It was her decision, and she left. Moving out of codependency means letting go. People have the right to live their life the way they want to, and all you can do is give them a choice, wish them well, and then let them go.

THE RESISTANT RECALCITRANT

Corey is an expert on all subjects. She is never without an opinion, and she is convinced that her point of view is right and non-negotiable. She differs from the Perennial Expert in that she is argumentative and combative. She is certain that life is tough and that at best you can maybe eke out a living, if you're lucky.

Corey was dealt a difficult hand from birth, and blames her parents for never understanding her. She was sent to all the wrong schools and insists that she was a special child, an artist, in fact, who needed individual attention and nurturing. Her energy was boundless and exhausting to watch. She required so much attention as an adult that she'd do anything to be the center of activity. She was so totally consumed by her own problems that she never listened to anyone else.

Corey was hired to arrange displays for an outdoor art show. At first her ideas were pretty good, and showed imagination and creativity. But Corey ran away with the project and neglected to obtain the artists' approval for certain expenditures. It became clear that she had no intention of collaborating with the other people on the project. She was a one-man band who took pride in making things happen, but she stepped on toes as regularly as a rank beginner learning to dance. Everyone grew angry at her and resentful of her clumsiness and insensitivity. For her part, Corey complained about being overworked, underpaid, and misunderstood. She never realized that she might have some role in the ongoing conflict which surrounded her.

THE RADIANT ROBOT

At first glance Lucy looked as if she had it all together. On closer examination however, it became apparent that she was a mass of insecurities. Lucy was in a sales and marketing consulting job for a major hotel chain. When she dealt with people, she came across as mechanical, preachy, and dogmatic because she had no ability to listen, and subsequently no ability to adapt her presentations to other people's needs. She was so self-absorbed that she could never win people over. There were many complaints from salespeople out in the field about Lucy because she looked good, but there seemed to be nobody home.

Finally, her manager sat down with her and addressed the issues. Lucy was told about the complaints that her staff and others had made about her, and she was asked for her responses. She communicated that she was very confused in her personal life, and didn't know if she was in the right job or even in the right city for her. She also said that she had come from a dysfunctional home in which her father was an alcoholic, and that she had always felt that she could never do a good enough job. She dressed up and paid excessive attention to how she looked so that no one would find out how inadequate she felt inside.

Lucy's manager encouraged her to take our company's Self Esteem/Inner Negotiation Workshop, which would allow her to find some inner strength and confi-

71

dence. She was also given the opportunity to participate in the employee assistance program in order to sort out her personal life and make some choices. Lucy chose to stay on the job, to find out what it meant to integrate her inner self with her public self, and to learn how to manage her staff.

THE ROOT OF NEGAHOLIC EMPLOYEE BEHAVIOR

Negaholic employees have most often been raised in dysfunctional homes. Having developed their dysfunctions in early childhood, they innocently bring them to their work environment as adults. In the office their problems become more pronounced, especially as they relate to relationships and tasks. Rather than looking at an employee and saying, "I don't know what is the matter with John. He has been acting strangely, and I don't know what to do with him," you can try to discover the origin of many of his behavior patterns and approach him in an intelligent way geared to produce positive results.

The following is a list of those behaviors originating from the dysfunctional home which are most often seen in negaholics on the job, no matter how high or low they are on the corporate ladder.

TEN TROUBLE SPOTS FOR NEGAHOLICS ON THE JOB

1. **Abandonment:** Fear of abandonment plagues people who were raised in dysfunctional homes. They may also feel left out, unimportant, or simply forgotten. Change-related activities, like promotions,

layoffs, acquisitions, mergers, buyouts, recognition, and awards, can all seriously affect the negaholic employee who suffers from fear of abandonment.

2. **Control:** People who were raised in dysfunctional homes often focus on control as an issue in their lives. They either felt no power and need to establish it now, or they felt out of control with no structure and are searching for some kind of stability. They may have been overly dominated or left to run wild, but as adults they frequently need to exert excessive control over their situations.

3. **Boundaries:** Having no or very porous personal boundaries, being unable to say "No," and feeling unable to differentiate between oneself, other people, the job, and situations is a classic characteristic of people from dysfunctional environments. In the work environment, this behavior translates into workaholism and an inability to set any sort of rational limits for oneself.

4. **Denial:** Avoiding or denying the reality of a situation is a learned behavior acquired from a dysfunctional home. In a work environment, this becomes evident in putting loyalties before telling the truth. It means internalizing issues rather than calling attention to them.

5. **Independence/Dependence:** Feeling a need for autonomy in the workplace is part of the reaction to being trapped in a dysfunctional home. At the same time, the person may also exhibit certain dependent behaviors. In other words, an individual may give off two contradictory messages: "Please take care of me," and "Get away from me, I can do it myself."

6. **Responsibility/Irresponsibility:** Either an overdeveloped sense of responsibility or an attitude of complete irresponsibility often makes up the nega-

holic personality. This is part of the binary existence of negaholics. Since they grew up in an unpredictable environment, and didn't know what would happen next, they often developed an excessive sense of responsibility. On the other hand, these people may choose to become totally irresponsible by opting out of the game completely.

7. **The need to be liked:** Since rejection and abuse were most probably a part of their dysfunctional past, negaholics will do anything to avoid more of the same. Having people like them and feeling loved are their top priorities. They become troubled if anyone openly displays dislike, and often will compromise themselves to win someone over.

8. **Authority issues:** There may be a push-pull relationship with authorities, in that the negaholic may be crying out for structure, boundaries, and definition, while at the same time rebelling against all authority figures as a carry-over from the past. If the authorities from childhood were not reliable, or let the person down, then there is probably a residue of anger and acting out that is triggered when authorities make demands in the workplace.

9. **The need for excitement, drama, and chaos:** Overstimulation is a way of life in the dysfunctional home, and so the negaholic employee is often in search of the adrenaline rush which enables him to feel alive and vital. He will often create crises, emergencies, traumas, calamities, and make major issues out of what appear to be simple concerns.

10. **Loyalties:** People from dysfunctional homes display extreme loyalty. Their loyalty can supersede their desire to be functional and healthy. Loyalty to a dysfunctional parent which is then transferred to an

unhealthy boss or organization will not serve the employee in the big picture.

SCREENING OUT NEGAHOLICS, OR SPOTTING DYSFUNCTIONS BEFORE THEY BECOME A PROBLEM

Before you hire a new employee, give him this information and then ask him the following questions. Listen for his answers in between the questions, and ask only one question at a time. Record all the information without making any snap judgments. You need to obtain the whole story before making any decisions.

♦ "I am looking for someone who matches the job, the people, and the environment here. I need someone who wants to make a long-term commitment to our company and grow with it. I want to find out if you are the right person for the job, given your personality, the type of work you enjoy, and the way you react to situations. I am going to ask you to tell me about yourself, honestly, and to share with me your decision-making process, what motivates you, what you enjoy and why, and what's most important to you. I want you to be honest, knowing that there is no wrong answer, but rather that I am looking for a person-job match. Tell me about your jobs, starting with the first job you ever had. Tell me what it was, why you chose it, what you liked about it, what you didn't care for, and why you left. Then go on to the second job, and so forth up to the present."

♦ "Now, tell me about your education. What did you like about school? Why? What didn't you like? Why?

What did you choose to study? Why? Why did you choose the schools you chose, and why did you stop when you did?"

♦ "How do you spend your spare time? When you are not busy doing your job, what interests you most, and what do you most enjoy doing?"

♦ "If I were to hire you, what would I recognize immediately as your strengths? What would gradually become apparent to me as your developmental needs? In other words, what areas do you want to develop, and how do you want to grow? What is important for me to know about you as a worker? Is there anything that you know of that might get in the way of you doing the job as I have outlined it today?"

After you have asked each question, listen and take notes. Listen to what prospectives say, what they don't say, and watch their body language. Notice when they maintain eye contact and when they look away. Notice when they seem to be inventing the right answer or trying to please you. Also be aware of any occasion when they volunteer the truth even if it sounds like the wrong thing to say. Your powers of observation are essential, and you want to pay attention to their tone, inflection, reactions, and responses. If you do this, you can conduct an effective interview and make a pretty accurate decision.

The next chapter tells you how to deal with negaholism between departments.

PART II

SITUATIONAL
OR
INTERDEPARTMENTAL
NEGAHOLISM

CHAPTER 4

◆

SITUATIONAL
OR INTERDEPARTMENTAL
NEGAHOLICS

When the various departments in your work environment interact, do they:

- Compete rather than collaborate?
- Appear to operate autonomously, not cooperatively?
- Have ambiguous if not strained relationships?
- Blame each other when things go wrong?
- Bicker and quarrel over what seem like trivial or childish issues?
- Appear isolated and pitted against each other by the department heads?
- Seem not to trust each other?
- Have breakdowns in communication where vital information is not transferred and knowledge is withheld as a territorial issue?
- Dwell on reasons, excuses, explanations, and justi-

fications rather than address the needed solutions?
♦ Display inconsistencies in direction, strategy, policies, or procedures?
♦ Have different or conflicting goals with respect to other departments or divisions?

If you answered "Yes" to any of these questions, then chances are that your company may be experiencing situational negaholism. Answering "Yes" does not mean that you yourself are a negaholic, or that your entire company is a negaholic corporation, but rather that it may have a localized strain of negaholism. This doesn't mean that the negaholism will not reverberate throughout the entire corporation, but rather that for now the contamination is localized between two work groups. Situational negaholism can occur between two departments, two divisions, the parent company and a subsidiary, or any two work groups which are at war with each other to the degree that it becomes a distraction. If the problem is pinpointed early enough, it can be cleared up efficiently and effectively before a full-blown negaholic epidemic occurs.

The first step is to take note of the dysfunctions in and around the organization and between its different departments. Just as a doctor uses a thermometer to take the patient's temperature or an armband to measure blood pressure, you need to establish a way to give your company a "physical" to assess its health before it contracts interdepartmental negaholism. It means paying attention to clues rather than ignoring them. When you hear subtle, snide, or sarcastic work-related comments, for example, listen to them as possible indicators of a serious problem. Don't gloss over them by saying, "Dave and Pete are always like that," or "All companies have problems between sales and service. It's always been that way and it always will be." Comments like these accept the dysfunctional signals as "normal" and deny the underlying problems.

When you notice that departments seem to be competing, say something about it, a simple comment like, "It seems to me that these two departments are in competition. Is that true, or am I seeing things unclearly?" If you notice that people seem not to trust each other, ask a question to find out whether that is true or not. When people seem to be consumed by problems, you might divert their attention to focusing on the solution. Just like the boy in "The Emperor's New Clothes" who said, "He's not wearing any clothes," you need to be willing to state the obvious in case everyone else is busy upholding the charade.

When you discount these signals, then you yourself become a part of the dysfunctional system. It is important to examine each symptom, explore the case history, and see if it applies to your current situation. The following are actual case histories, drawn from our experience as management consultants, which show how the symptoms manifest themselves.

COMPETE RATHER THAN COLLABORATE

Barry was the chief financial officer of a multinational holding company which had holdings in over forty countries worldwide. Recently, his job had changed from CFO to chief operating officer. As the COO, he had over forty thousand people reporting to him. Barry viewed his job as the mainstay of the company. His function was to ensure that whatever was already in existence would continue to exist and flourish. He thought of himself as essential to the effective functioning of the company.

Clint was the director of all new products and programs. His responsibilities included organization, planning, research and development, recruitment of new key personnel, and all other activities having to do with the future. Clint enjoyed his job and perceived his role as that of an innovator who could save the company from stagnation.

Clint and Barry did not get along. Each thought that the other was superfluous and uninteresting. They competed for the attention and approval of the CEO, Darrell. As leaders, each mobilized his staff against the other's. The groups withheld information from each other, plotted, schemed, and became preoccupied with undermining the opposing team. Naturally, doing business became a sideline activity; since the "enemy" was within the ranks, it was a full-time job just defending and protecting one's own turf.

I was one of a team of consultants who worked with this mammoth company. It was a difficult assignment because the company asked for help, but in truth really didn't want to change any of its old behaviors. In order for me to work with a client effectively, he has to be willing to examine his own behaviors in terms of their impact on those around him. He has to be willing to make some changes in order for the desired results to be produced. In this particular situation, Barry, Clint, and Darrell were locked into old patterns which they were not willing to give up. Sadly, they are still at it today.

ARE INCONSISTENCIES RELATED TO DIRECTION, STRATEGY, POLICIES, OR PROCEDURES?

A large, publicly-held conglomerate had purchased several midsize businesses in the southeastern part of the United States. Les, who had previously owned the businesses but had sold them, was now a high-level executive of the parent company. After the acquisition was complete, Les decided that the parent company was improperly managed, and that because of this mismanagement he wasn't getting a good enough return on his investment. He was at odds with Wilbur, the CEO, and decided that the only way to regain his hold on the company was through stock acquisition. He set out on a mission to cast suspicion upon the CEO's leadership abilities. His strategy was to undermine Wilbur's credibility so that the board's trust in him would be eroded, which would in turn enable Les and the board to replace him.

Les embarked upon his strategy to unseat Wilbur in a very methodical manner. He bought up stock aggressively, and after he had amassed approximately 11 percent of the total available stock, he secured himself a seat on the board of directors. Then he started leaking information to the press: the company was poorly managed, and because of the unwise decisions that were being made, the company was losing its market share. He sought every opportunity to get his name into the press, to increase his visibility, and to cast doubt on Wilbur's leadership. He began lobbying the former CEO, Grant, by casually and frequently suggesting that Wilbur was inadequate for the scope of the task, and indeed the wrong person for the job altogether. He strove to undermine Grant's confidence in Wilbur. It was a case of corporate sabotage. He lobbied other board members. At a certain point, he and his allies controlled twenty-five percent of the total public stock. His strategy was working. As profits slid, Wilbur's confidence began to erode as well.

Wilbur started vacillating. Calls from analysts soliciting information for investor relations made him anxious. He made decisions, then within days or weeks reversed them. He started doubting himself. He had lost his conviction, his certainty, his confidence. He was losing his constituency and his grasp on reality. At times he thought he was losing his mind. A strong and competent leader was deteriorating into a nervous, paranoid, uncertain, fearful shell of a man. Ultimately, Les was successful. It took six months to do the dirty deed, but Wilbur was finally ousted and Grant, the former CEO, was reinstated.

During this six-month period, consultants were brought in by Wilbur to study different aspects of the company. Consultants studied the budgets, the structure, reporting systems, marketing, operations, the validity of different departments, the use of space, the effectiveness of programs, and anything else that could be analyzed. Since the leadership at the top was shaky, the reverberations could be felt throughout the organization. Programs were initiated and within three months canceled. New space was acquired, redesigned, and then abandoned. New systems were purchased and developed, then canceled. Decisions were impulsive, compulsive, and off the wall. Issues were insufficiently researched and inadequately thought out in terms of the long-range consequences. Expensive decisions were being made daily. The organization reflected the insecurities of the CEO, as well as the power struggle between Les and Wilbur.

CORPORATE QUAKE

After Grant replaced Wilbur, a search was conducted for a new CEO. A person was found, but he lasted less than a year. Within four years, four different CEOs, each with different management styles, priorities, procedures, and processes, contributed to the corporate quake. The frequent change of leaders created organizational vertigo, and people were uncertain from day to day whether they were coming or going. From the laissez-faire style of management to the "Thou shalt do what I command" approach, employees were caught in the tumult of revolving-door management. Profits dropped from twenty-eight dollars per share to under seven.

Because of the lack of consistent leadership, clear vision, and an alignment of all the key players, the bottom line suffered terribly. This was a case of egos running wild. Despite attempts to control the situation, no one could stop the company's downward spiral. Since there was a lack of commitment to dealing with the dysfunctional behaviors—that is, the conspiracy, the undermining, the sabotage, and the premeditated fall of the designated leader—there was no way to make the company healthy again. This was a clear case of situational negaholism. One person's desires and aspirations eclipsed the organizational strategy, purpose, and mission, and affected the lives of tens of thousands of employees.

APPEAR TO OPERATE AUTONOMOUSLY, NOT COOPERATIVELY

Tony, a heavyset plodder in his mid-fifties, a colorless man who blends into environments so that you hardly ever notice him, has a department of eight people who report to him. He lives within the rules of the organization and displays virtually no creativity of his own. When he gets embarrassed, his chin starts to quiver—this is the most extreme reaction that you'll ever see from Tony. No matter what his ten direct subordinates request, his answer is the same: it can't happen. Regardless of whether they want a stamp pad or more pens, the answer is either perennial procrastination or a flat "No." There is an underlying, unspoken law in his department that people should never take vacations. Continual complaints about the antiquated systems have become part of the liturgy. Decisions are made without group consensus. He has very little empathy, and cannot relate to the problems and concerns of his staff. His "open door policy" is rather a joke, since his employees feel that they will either get trapped in the den of negativity or have the open door slammed shut in their faces. The staff has learned how to work around him, to avoid contact at all costs, and to get the job done in spite of him.

Marguerite works day and night to keep the salespeople on their toes selling more and more print jobs. She is constantly overwhelmed, and is much too busy to teach her staff of ten anything she is doing. She needs to have contact with everything, and unless she has her fingers in every pie, she is unhappy. Marguerite believes that she does things the right way, and she is too old a dog to even consider new tricks. There is only one way to do things, and that is Marguerite's way. As soon as staff members can transfer out of her domain, they do. The culture abounds with long-term irreconcilable misunderstandings.*

Tony, the manager of the print shop, is in charge of

---

* A culture is a system of beliefs and actions that characterize a particular group. Culture is the shared ideas, customs, assumptions, expectations, philosophy, traditions, mores, values, and understandings that determine how a group of people will behave. When one talks about a corporation's culture, one is referring to the complex, interrelated, standardized, institutionalized, habitual behavior that characterizes that firm and that firm only. In some ways culture can be thought of as a corporation's self-concept, and is analogous to the idea of an individual's personality. Culture develops over a long period of time, although its fundamental elements are often established during an organization's early years.

ad production. He is responsible for all the ads arriving on time and being properly presented so that they can be incorporated into the magazine layout. He wears white short-sleeved shirts, and his thin mustache feels the aftershocks of his quivering chin.

The print schedule was off. Commitments were being missed, and Tony and Marguerite were locked in a hostile confrontation. The sales force and the printers were at odds. There was no format for handling differences of opinion. Old problems were left unresolved, and the salespeople were constantly challenged by the printing staff, who mirrored Tony's "It can't happen" attitude. There was uncertainty about charting the work flow, and a conflict between the salaried workers in one department and the wage-earners in the other. The printers were feelers and the salespeople were thinkers. When a printing job was well done, it was taken for granted, ignored, and brushed aside by Tony. Both departments observed their managers' territorial behavior and mirrored it.

Harry, the head of both the print shop and the sales department, approached our firm with this situation. After hearing all the symptoms, we knew that the issues had to be put on the table and addressed by all the players. People had to discuss their frustrations both at the relationship level as well as in terms of strategizing task orientation. We met with all the people individually and synthesized their responses into a diagnostic report that was fed back to management. The consensus was to have a team-building day in which issues, concerns, and problems were openly addressed in a safe and controlled environment where we could focus on solutions and results. People were summoned to rise above their quarrels and grievances, transcend their differences, and formulate win-win solutions.

During the team-building day, the two departments, the sales force and the printing staff, explored what needed to happen in order for each to respect the other. Both departments became committed to creating a genuine team spirit from scratch. There was a shift in focus from pointing out mistakes and rubbing them in to making needed corrections and learning important lessons. The following communication strategies were articulated to employees of each department:

1. Ask questions to clarify requests. Understanding another person's perspective will help you make good assessments.
2. Validate people's input by acknowledging their participation. Remember that this is a valuable way to discover what you need to know about your department.
3. Avoid "no" as a knee-jerk response. If you find yourself wanting to say a flat-out "No," get together with a member of the team and explore the validity of the request before you respond.
4. Consider all requests in light of the objectives and the purpose of the project. This will clarify the decision-making process.

When Marguerite was privately interviewed, she wondered whether Tony were reminiscent of any other person in her life. She searched her memory, and up popped the image of her ex-husband, with whom she had very little in common. As with her ex-husband, Marguerite could never get the result she wanted from Tony when she requested it, and she was infuriated every time this happened. She was convinced that he had been out to get her. They worked at different speeds, and this was a real source of aggravation. She found that, in the dance of life, they were continuously on each other's toes.

Marguerite and Tony developed a buzz-word to remind themselves of the new relationship they were in the process of building. However, after many painstaking sessions, Tony's boss said, "Tony has demoralized the group and I don't know if he can be turned around." Eventually he was offered an early retirement, which he accepted happily. The path to harmony is paved with hard work every day. In this instance, the employees' needs were taken seriously and management's commitment to them was demonstrated in full.

HAVE AN AMBIGUOUS IF NOT STRAINED RELATIONSHIP BECAUSE OF LACK OF TRUST, AND ARE UNCLEAR WHETHER TO INTERFACE OR NOT, OR IF SO, HOW

Doug was the head of the sales department. He was well-educated and was taking courses to complete his MBA. He was people-oriented, a positive thinker, and eager to do a good job. The people in his department mirrored his leadership and followed suit as up-tempo, enthusiastic salespeople. More than anything they loved closing sales, and they were successful in doing so.

Doug had a problem which was beginning to bother him more and more. He felt that the service department was lazy and unresponsive to customer needs. Other people had noticed this too. The real problem was that the service department was too backed up to service the accounts it already had, and the logjam was affecting the sales department's ability to sell more systems. The complaints were affecting customer service and giving the sales department a bad name.

Fred was a dedicated technician who had worked his way up from systems installer to head of the service department. He was thorough and knew the technical aspects of his job, but he was never trained to manage people. He backed his people up and defended them when they were criticized, but he was unfamiliar with how to collaborate with a peer and tackle a problem nondefensively but head-on. Fred could be counted on to get the job done and done right. He was a self-made guy, extremely proud, who had difficulty asking anyone for support. His thinking was logical and literal, and he did everything by the book.

Fred thought that all salespeople were alike. They had no technical skills and would sell anything, even products which couldn't be delivered. They would tell the customer anything that might close the sale, and then dump the impossible order in the service department's lap. In short, Fred thought salespeople were only out for their commissions. The service people, on the other hand, had the real job to do. They had to make the system work, and it wasn't easy. But whether the job was relatively easy or really tough, they got paid the same: their salary. There were no bonuses for the service person who figured out how to install a huge multidimensional system, but if a salesperson sold a huge system, he saw the result in his commission check. What galled Fred was that service did all the work!

Every time Doug came to Fred with a problem about the service department filling orders, Fred became defensive and protective about his staff and its per-

formance. He couldn't stand listening to Doug's unjus-
tified complaints about his overworked and underpaid
staff. He felt that his staff was already doing cartwheels
to accommodate the unrealistic demands of the sales
staff.

Doug, on the other hand, had little sympathy for the
service group. All day long he heard complaints concerning their confusion about orders, their lateness in
filling requests, and their bungling of existing orders.
His point of view was that his salespeople were "bust-
ing their butts" to make money for the corporation,
while the lazy service bums sat around and chewed the
fat all day.

This was clearly a case of interdepartmental negaholism. There was no alignment between sales and service, and little or no communication. Instead, there
were conspiracies, subterfuges, and secrets.

When we met with Fred and Doug, we introduced
them to the notion that differences could be viewed as
an asset rather than a liability. We let them know that
unless service and sales worked together, the customer
would ultimately be the one to suffer. If the customer
were sacrificed, then everyone would lose. The alternative action was to look at the inequities and the resentments and find solutions which would create a win-win
outcome. Unless everyone wins, no one really wins.
Fred and Doug finally acknowledged that it would be
better if the salespeople were committed to making the
jobs and lives of the service people easier, and vice
versa. Now, with the focus on support rather than competition or sabotage, the game changed radically. The
foremost goal had to be: "What can I do to support you?
How can I make your life easier?" This way, *all* would
feel a sense of accomplishment and completion if every-

body won. The new approach included verbal support. Each department vowed to stop agreeing with the customer about how its counterpart was wrong. Encountering criticisms and complaints, both were now committed to getting to the bottom of the issue and turning the customer around.

BICKER AND QUARREL OVER WHAT SEEM LIKE TRIVIAL OR CHILDISH ISSUES

A chain of electronics stores was experiencing an accelerated growth pattern, but a conflict between the sales and marketing departments threatened to escalate into disaster. Called in as an adviser, I first talked with Suzanna, a manager in the marketing department. Suzanna was despondent. Things, she said, just weren't working out:

"The head of our department is completely out of touch with his work group. He is cold, aloof, and distant. The employees complain that they can't talk to him. He doesn't understand what goes on around here, and he thinks he's on top of everything. Marketing can't get the results that they want, and worse, marketing is blaming sales for not returning their calls. Marketing spends untold hours designing and dreaming up ads for the stores that the stores then complain about. The stores say marketing doesn't understand the products, and even if the ads hit the papers in time, there isn't enough product in the stores to support the cost of the ads," Suzanna said in disbelief.

"Suzanna, what do you think is at the root of all this?" I asked inquisitively.

"The field (sales) doesn't have a clear understanding of marketing's responsibilities. But, by the same to-ken, marketing doesn't know what the salespeople do out in the field. Then there is the ongoing saga of inventory control. There's never enough product to meet the demand. The marketing department does not always inform sales about its promotions and often appears to be unclear about its priorities. Our goals seem to be the same, but the interpretation of those goals by sales and marketing is totally different. We can't figure out whether the company is market-driven or sales-driven. There is no internal support for the staff. When a staff member is absent, the entire department comes to a halt."

"It sounds like there are some serious issues which pertain to job definition, responsibilities, priorities, and alignment," I said, trying to sum it up.

"I think it goes even deeper than that. As a member of the marketing department, I don't think that the sales force trusts us. So when we make recommendations, they discount them," she said with emotion.

"Suzanna, keep going. It sounds like this is starting to crystallize," I said encouragingly.

"I think there is a power struggle between sales and marketing. There is no feeling of cooperation and collaboration. It's as if we're in competition. It seems like marketing is the old traditional way of doing things, and sales is run by the new kids who have no credentials to back them up. This is so nutty! The marketing department is comprised of people who have gone to school and have MBAs. The sales force is for the most part right out of school—they know how to use their wits, but have no formal sales education. They operate mostly by the seat of their pants, just out there selling like crazy. Rather than appreciating our knowledge and expertise, they resent us. They even insinuate that we sit in our ivory tower, dreaming up good ideas, and are virtually out of touch with the needs of the public. I can't believe that we have two departments that are supposed to work so closely, yet that are so far apart. It sounds pretty crazy, doesn't it?"

"Suzanna, before I comment, tell me how you feel about all of this."

"Frustrated and misunderstood. You'd think we were the enemy! I know that ultimately we all need to sit down together with a facilitator and sort out these issues, but I don't think sales would ever go along with it. They'd accuse us of trying to shrink their heads. Besides, I don't know how sales and marketing can become a team when marketing can't even agree that there is a problem. Marketing thinks this is normal. They think that the tension between marketing and sales is an age-old problem that will never go away. I have to convince them that there is another way of doing business."

"So what do we do?" I asked with interest.

"I think I have to set up a meeting with my boss and see what he says about the situation. I've been talking about team-building for six months, and I think he may be ready to make some decisions. Things are not working the way he envisioned."

A meeting was called with Toby, who was the head of the marketing department, in which he agreed to an internal team-building effort with the marketing department alone. We would thrash out the internal concerns and come to an agreement among ourselves before even considering including sales in a joint session.

During the meeting, the marketing staff agreed on how little management support it experienced from

Toby. Toby became defensive, saying that he wanted to work with adults and had no desire to take part in the daily squabbles. He said he didn't want to participate in the whining and complaining that went on in the department, and wanted them to figure out a way to work out their issues among themselves.

It was a difficult session. Toby's laissez-faire form of management was antithetical to the demands set forth by the staff. As people started opening up, the emotional temperature rose in the room. People started talking about what mattered to them. It became clear that they needed to tackle some significant questions before they put in one more day without a sense of mission, purpose, and focused alignment.

"Toby, the people in the department simply do not support each other," Cheryl said. "When I discussed my workload with you, Toby, you told me to go ask Cindy. When I asked her for back-up support, Cindy told me that it wasn't in her job description and she didn't have time."

"If you guys can't work it out, we're in trouble. We're all adults here. This is like a quarrel between children and I don't want to be your father," Toby said in an exasperated tone. "If you can't figure it out, I just don't know what to say." He was distant and aloof.

After having observed the manner in which Toby interacted with his employees, I felt it was time to have a meeting with Toby to find out how he viewed the situation. We scheduled a time to meet when we would have no interruptions or distractions. The next day, Toby asked me for my observations of the meeting.

"There was something about what Carol said, or the way she said it, that seemed to rub you the wrong way. What was it?" I asked.

95

"I'm not exactly sure. She's such a whiner. No matter how much time I give her, it's never enough," he said with a sigh.

"You did appear to have a rather short fuse," I said matter-of-factly.

"She is one of my biggest problems. Did you ever work with a person who complained and whined and just generally drove you crazy?" he asked.

"I've been around people like that, if that's what you mean," I said.

"Were my feelings really obvious?" he asked.

"Obvious to me, because I saw how tolerant you were with the other employees. She really hits a nerve. Would you be interested in finding another way to interact with her by looking at what other issues your short fuse might be wired to?" I inquired.

Toby's eagerness to resolve the issues between marketing and sales resulted in a meaningful discussion which revealed some important facts. I asked him what he felt when Carol "whined" at him.

"Frustrated, upset, and angry," he said after a long silence. "Feelings aren't my strong suit."

"I understand," I said emphatically. "Do you feel that way around other members of the staff?"

"Only the women. The men seem to be able to handle their own problems and reconcile their differences. I feel like a dad with a bunch of kids. Each time there is an issue with any of the women, they always come to me to referee. I can't stand spending my time that way. I like to think I'm working with adults, not petulant children," he said.

"Tell me more about the feeling of frustration," I asked. "Where do you feel it?"

"In my stomach," he said. "It gets tight and I feel sick."

"Is there anybody else who gives you that same feeling?" I pressed.

"Yeah, I feel that same way around Terri, my girl-friend. Every time she brings up the subject of commitment I have the same sick feeling in my stomach," he said.

"Tell me more about her."

"She works for the company, and everybody knows that it's not a great idea to have a relationship with someone in the same company. Besides, she keeps harping at me that I'm so unemotional and detached. I don't know what she wants from me exactly, but whatever I do it's never enough for her," he mused.

"It sounds as if there may be a parallel between Terri and your department that's similar to what some of your staff were saying in the meeting. Carol wants more direction and Terri wants more attention. They both seem to want more from you, at least more than you are willing to give. Does that sound right to you? Toby, can you recreate the feeling that you experience when Terri says you're unemotional or detached?"

"Yeah, I can feel it, and I don't like it," he said.

"Does this feeling remind you of any other similar experience?" I nudged.

"It reminds me of when I was a kid, but I don't want to talk about that."

"You don't have to if you don't want to," I said consolingly.

"I don't know what that has to do with my job," he said.

"What is the 'that'? Will you tell me what you're thinking?" I asked.

"I was the only boy out of six kids. My mother and I were really close. I don't know what happened, but one day she just went away. After several weeks, they told us she had had a nervous breakdown. I felt responsible for my sisters and I had to pick up the slack for my mother when she was gone. When she came back she was a changed person, and we never got to have the same closeness after she returned. We never filled in the year that was lost," he said as his eyes welled up with tears.

"How do you feel about that now?"

"Emotional and upset."

"Is there anything else about this time that you want to say?" I asked.

"I thought it was all buried for so long, but the feelings I have around Carol are just like the ones I got from all the demands my sisters put on me. I can still feel the pressure of all the responsibilities I assumed after Mom left. When I come to think of it, I was a father at thirteen," he said with surprise.

"It sounds like some of these realizations could be illuminating in your work situation. Perhaps your childhood relationship with your sisters is carrying over to your relationships with women in general. It sounds as if you may have made a decision back in your formative years that women always want more from you than you can give. If this is true, then your relationships with Terri, Carol, and in fact with your whole department are a reenactment of the relationship you had with your five younger sisters," I said, summarizing. "It is curious that your whole department consists of women."

Toby was visibly shaken. He had awakened a memory which had been buried in the corners of his mind. Using a recent feeling as a starting point, he had traced it back through time to its source in a childhood experience. That original experience had made a lasting imprint on his mind, and was the filter through which he viewed all women who were related to him. Toby's self-discovery shed a whole new light on his present circumstances. When the newness of the emotion had subsided, I asked him what he wanted to do about the past, and the present. He said that he wanted to contact each one of his sisters and start the process of healing the old relationships. He wanted to end the burden, the pressure, and the feelings of inadequacy of trying to be a parent to five younger sisters. "Besides," he said, "I'm carrying around such old stuff. It's time to let go of it." It was not going to be quick and easy, but he was determined to start the process.

On the job, he now wanted to take note of each time feelings surfaced which reminded him of his past relationships with his sisters. In addition, Toby agreed to tell Carol that she reminded him of Sara, his younger sister, and what that meant to him. As a result of that conversation their working relationship was permanently changed for the better. They never again felt the strain and tension which had previously marked their relationship. The tension disappeared completely. He also decided to tell his girlfriend about his discoveries in the hope that the self-disclosure would draw them even closer. He hoped that it would help her understand him better. As a result of the conversation between Terri and Toby, their relationship was altered and went to a deeper level.

APPEAR ISOLATED AND PITTED AGAINST ONE ANOTHER BY THE DEPARTMENT HEADS

A public relations firm with two partners at the helm was run like a family. Henry and Bob had been partners for many years. They knew how to work with and around each other. Henry was never satisfied with anything. Whenever a program was presented to him, he would invariably find something wrong with it. The kindest thing he could say was "O.K." He was a terrible listener, full of judgments, and by nature was explosive. Most often, when people would tell him something he would blow up.

Bob was the antithesis of Henry, understanding and compassionate. The staff knew that it could always come to Bob with its problems. He was a warm person with an open mind. Bob was the nurturer who showed that he really cared about his people.

Staff members would joke about the Mommy/Daddy relationship they had with Henry and Bob. You go to Daddy when you have to give the status of your project, and after Daddy yells at you, you go to Mommy to have your wounds licked and be healed from the battle. Everyone feared going to Henry, and conversely loved talking to Bob. Henry and Bob never resolved their situation. They continued to blame their high employee turnover rate on the young people of today and on the world situation. They were never sufficiently motivated to find out if anything in their management style drove people away. Miraculously, they are still in business, but things haven't changed.

Interestingly enough, every member of the staff had had a similar situation in childhood, with one good and one bad parent. Either the mother was the nurturer and the father was the mean guy, or vice versa. Staff members played out their childhood issues with their parents in the form of Henry and Bob. The family scenario went on and on. Without an intervention, these family dynamics would go on indefinitely. It seemed so amazingly normal that no one thought a problem existed.

The company is still around today, still plagued with a high turnover rate and the same old communication breakdowns. Henry and Bob continue to play out their traditional roles, and the staff still continues to snicker as well as act out its role as the children in the corporate family. Since Bob and Henry are so good at what they do, and since people are always looking for jobs in P.R., the system will continue. Just as dysfunctional families pass the legacy from one generation to the next, dysfunctional companies pass their dysfunctions on from one generation of employees to the next.

HAVE BREAKDOWNS IN COMMUNICATION WHERE VITAL INFORMATION IS NOT TRANSFERRED AND KNOWLEDGE IS WITHHELD AS A WEAPON AND A TERRITORIAL ISSUE

A large hospital chain was dealing with breakdowns in communication. Merely on principle, departments did not talk to other departments. Human resources and the public relations departments had to work very closely together, because human resources was designing programs to develop the staff while the public relations department had to frame the new programs so that they were newsworthy. Much communication had to take place between the two groups in order for the objectives to be reached. Both internal and external communication had to be aligned in order to produce results. Every time they had to collaborate on a project, however, for instance the design of the new employee orientation program, the two departments would disagree. They would argue about purpose, philosophy, methods, strategy, approach, process, content, and style, until finally the whole meeting would blow up. People from both departments would storm off, frustrated and muttering comments about the "other" group.

Upon closer inspection, it became evident that there was more going on than meets the eye. The head of the public relations department, Ann, was having an affair with Roger, the chairman of the board. The head of the human resources department felt uninformed about plans and threatened by Ann's relationship with Roger. The two leaders galvanized their work groups into two armed camps which worked in direct opposition to each other. They couldn't agree on anything. Things would either be ignored, get canceled, or be done badly. There was so much polarization, egocentrism, and righteousness that either group would lose face if it waved the white flag.

There were certain people who wanted our expertise and knowledge to help transform the situation. Those people felt that we could help the situation, but those in charge didn't want outsiders finding out certain information. Since they were dealing with secret, taboo topics, and in general were avoiding the real issue, there was little chance of resolving the breakdowns in communication. Discussing these issues was too threatening for the culture to handle.

DWELL ON REASONS, EXCUSES, EXPLANATIONS, AND JUSTIFICATIONS RATHER THAN ADDRESS THE NEEDED SOLUTIONS

A top publishing company with one of the best reputations in the business had contracted a mild case of negaholism. Jason's novel had to be published, but with all the buck-passing, people were starting to wonder. The production department was behind, the art director was late on the cover design, the typesetters hadn't completed the typesetting, and the galleys were supposed to be sent out last week. Everything was late and the job simply wasn't getting done. The domino effect was in full swing. The designer blamed the editor. The editor blamed the author. The production department blamed the typesetters, and the typesetters blamed the editor for not getting the final edited copy back to them.

No one took responsibility for the book getting published. Everyone on the project had reasons and excuses as to why he couldn't get his job done. No one was willing to stop the machinery and say that he had a role in the ripple effect. Everyone was a cog in the totally nonproductive grand machine. No one person was willing to take charge of the situation.

Finally, the publisher had to resort to threats of severe consequences in order to get any results. The publisher got the job done, but not without undue stress and hassle. She asked herself, "Does it always have to be such an ordeal?"

DEPARTMENTS WITH CONFLICTING GOALS

Ted, the sales director for a major communications company, is soft-spoken, people-oriented, and a living example of a "Theory Y" manager. As defined by Douglas McGregor, who coined the term, a Theory Y manager operates under several basic assumptions: the expenditure of physical and mental effort is natural; external control and the threat of punishment are not the only means of bringing about organizational objectives; commitment to objectives is a function of the rewards associated with their achievement; the average person learns, under proper conditions, not only to accept responsibility but to seek it out; the capacity to exercise a relatively high degree of imagination, ingenuity, and creativity in the solution of organizational problems is widely distributed throughout the population; and, under the conditions of modern industrial life, the intellectual potential of the average human being is only partially utilized.

Ted had to work with Bob, a play-it-safe company man. Ted was entrepreneurial by nature and had his own company before coming on board. He enjoyed taking risks and playing for high stakes, but the offer he received from his old friend, Ed, was so irresistible that he decided to join corporate America.

Each director represented the sales division of two separate companies which were owned by the same parent company. Bob was the general sales director in the parent company and Ted was the sales director in the subsidiary company. On the surface they were friendly good ol' boys who played golf together and chatted about the latest ball scores, but underneath their camaraderie lay a protective distancing. A definite tension surfaced every time the subject of the two sales forces was addressed. Things became so bad that management decided outside help was needed, and called us in. Incredibly enough, there seemed to be conflict between the two sales forces.

Ted wanted to get to the heart of the matter and clear up the conflicting issues between the two sales groups, while Bob was committed to maintaining the status quo. "Leave well enough alone" was his motto.

After having interviewed each member of the two sales forces, we discovered a great deal of secrecy on the part of the two companies, and little collaboration between them on client contact, referrals, or follow-up. After some digging, we discovered that there were two totally different compensation plans which remunerated the employees in completely different ways. Each company was actively selling different communication systems in direct competition to its sister company. In addition, each company interpreted governmental rules and regulations in slightly different ways. The bottom line was that the charter objectives of the two companies were in conflict.

The subsidiary company had recently been started up as an entrepreneurial arm of the old, bureaucratic telecommunications firm. People were handpicked from the parent company to form the subsidiary. The people who were selected were told that "only the cream of the crop" had been chosen, and as a result they felt special and important. Conversely, those who were not chosen and who stayed at the parent company harbored a lot of resentment toward their "'chosen" counterparts. Those pioneers who formed the subsidiary were led to believe that they could do no wrong, and that there were unlimited resources for their development as a new entity. Right from the start, there was an inherent conflict.

The situation was similar to that of a parent who has raised a family, divorced, remarried, and had a new baby. The baby is adored by its parents and subsequently resented by the children of the previous marriage. The older children, who were raised with strict rules, curfews, and a limited budget when times were tough, feel excessive animosity toward the newcomer. Watching the baby get all the attention, affection, and

105

unconditional love is agonizing to the older children. The schism between the generations within the family widens as the resentment grows. Similarly, the two sales departments acted like families who know they are stuck with each other and have no choice in the matter.

CORPORATE MUSICAL CHAIRS

The conflict between the two sales departments was very real. Competition was built into the system and acted out by the sales forces, which would joust with each other for the hand of the fair maiden, the customer. Each company sold similar equipment in direct competition with the other. The compensation plans were different, and on top of it all the respective charter objectives of the two companies were in conflict. There were secrets between the two companies and little real communication. If the sales forces were to be combined, there would be a game of musical chairs, with too many bodies trying to fill too few seats.

We decided to hold a meeting on the problem. Sitting down at the table to address these issues felt almost like committing a crime. Secrets are secrets because you only discuss them in whispers behind people's backs. You are not supposed to discuss them openly. Addressing secrets means reversing the dysfunction and becoming functional. Each group was sheepish and withdrawn, not wanting to admit to its own dysfunctional behaviors.

The cat was out of the bag. We had been brought in to help the organization become healthy. We were now asking the two groups to discuss the unspeakable. We were asking them to confront the unconfrontable. We were asking them to reveal, admit, and deal with what wasn't working. We asked them if it were possible to collaborate and cooperate. We probed for solutions to age-old problems. We pressed them to go beyond their natural inclinations, to argue for their limitations, and to go for what they really wanted: a healthy organization in which people worked together in a productive and honest way.

Each issue was laid on the table. We looked at what the specific, tangible desired end result for each issue would be. Then we discussed what was needed in the way of obtaining the desired result. Possible solutions were brainstormed, and all the options were considered. After the first flush of nega-babble—what wouldn't work and why different options couldn't work—we discussed what could work, and what we were willing to do about it. A master plan was mapped out and people chose their parts. We had a battle plan, an army that had bought in to the vision, and the commitment to make it happen. The results were remarkable.

It wasn't the groups' intelligence that made it happen. It wasn't their ingenuity that drove it home. It wasn't their marketing skills that bred success. It was their absolute, undaunted commitment which brought about the desired results. The dysfunctional behavior was dismantled and substituted with functional, healthy behavior.

HOW TO DEAL WITH CHANGE IN A FUNCTIONAL WAY

All of the above situations involved some sort of change. If you are going to take a dysfunctional aspect of your company and make it fully functional and healthy, then you must plan on bringing about significant changes in behavior patterns. Changes in attitudes, changes in the culture, and changes in behavior patterns all require deliberate design as well as knowledge of human response. A "change" process could mean changing the culture, the structure, the policies, the systems, the procedures, the staff, or any other aspect which affects people's lives. If you design or engineer change, you need to understand and be prepared for the human reaction to change, and know how to deal with it.

With change come disruption, disorientation, and some disorganization. People become comfortable in their environments when things are predictable, stable, and within their control. When they know what is expected of them, people tend to relax. They may not be happy, but they are comfortable. It is important to note that there is a clear distinction between comfortable and happy. "Comfort" is associated with ease and well-being, while "happy" is associated with pleasure, joy, or contentment. A person may be very comfortable in a job he has had for fifteen years, but he may not be very happy. Comfort relates to how a person has constructed his frame of reference.

An individual's frame of reference is an unconscious composite of thoughts, feelings, perceptions, attitudes, beliefs, values, assumptions, experiences, and behaviors which comprise his general orientation to the world. It is how and why he does what he does. His frame of reference is amorphous and gives him a sense of security bred of familiarity, predictability, and control. When you disrupt a person's frame of reference, you distort his psychological equilibrium. You dislodge one of the linchpins which holds his reality in place. How radical the change process determines how intense the recipient's emotional vertigo.

Before the change has occurred, the recipient is most likely in a fairly stable state. His world is familiar, predictable, controllable, and safe. He knows who he is, what to expect, and what is expected of him. There are very few, if any, surprises. When you introduce the element of change, you bring in the unknown. With the unknown comes the uncertain, the unpredictable, the unstable, and the uncontrolled. Things are no longer familiar, but foreign. What was once comfortable has now become uncomfortable. People are confused and disoriented by the change process. Along with their confusion bubble up a myriad of feelings which may range from exhilaration to anxiety, from anticipation to loss, from anger to sadness, from denial to depression.

Some people respond to the change process with excitement and anticipation. These are the ones who thrive on change. They are the entrepreneurs, the type "A" personalities, the risk-takers who are motivated partly by a desire to avoid boredom. The large majority of people, however, avoid and fear change. They want their world the way it was, and will do almost anything to void disruption. The last thing they want is a life-quake or an identity crisis.

When a change occurs, people are often unconscious of the degree of their attachment to one frame of reference. Psychologically speaking, they may understand the change, but they don't comprehend why they feel the way they do. Their malaise or irritability seems unaccounted for, and they mentally punish themselves for not being on top of it all. Changes wreak havoc on our emotions. Even if we don't like to admit it, change can

109

have a devastating effect on our emotional, psychological, and physical well-being.

In an organization undergoing a change process, management's lack of attention to the effect it will have upon the employees can result in disaster. From an office move to becoming computerized, from changing a product line to rapid, intense growth, from dramatic changes in personnel to mergers, acquisitions, and leveraged buy-outs, change has far-reaching, profound effects on those whose lives it touches.

Change affects people on many levels. The first level, the physical, is the most immediate. The desk gets moved, the papers get signed, the people board the plane. You can see it, hear it, smell it, and touch it.

The psychological level is second in terms of impact. The person must stop taking the same old route to work, he must remember to turn to the terminal instead of grabbing a pad and pen, or he must adjust to the fact that the office is not like the close-knit family that it used to be. This is the level of cognition, of awareness. The physical reality is becoming integrated into the mental computer and then ultimately into the behavior patterns.

The third level, and the most challenging to manage, is the emotional. The emotional level is the least tangible. When people are affected emotionally by change, a whole series of past events comes to the surface. The person feels the effects of the present situation as well as the residue of unresolved issues from the past. For instance, when a person is laid off due to a merger or an acquisition, he may feel the loss of separation from his present situation because it means saying goodbye to old friends and to a job he may have liked. It may mean the loss of good feelings and a special cup of coffee at break time, or a favorite place to have a croissant. It may be a familiar traffic pattern, a view of the water, or the friendly "Hello" from old Jake, the security guard. The nostalgia of saying goodbye to those fond memories when you yourself didn't initiate the change has greater impact than if and when you did.

At the same time, change may revive incidents from the employee's past, when he was involuntarily separated from those whom he loved. The result may be a flood of emotions. The response appears to be disproportionate to the stimulus, and in fact it is. The triggering effect has called forth not only professional losses but personal ones as well. There may be memories of changing schools, moving to a different city, or of a dear old dog who died. The emotions cannot differentiate between personal and professional scars; they simply record the trauma. Upon stimulation of a similar emotion, the entire chain of related emotional experiences is triggered.

Take, for example, a business which, innocently enough, plans to computerize its operation and is met with massive resistance from the employees. Unaware of the impact of the decision and of its effect on the staff, management proceeds blindly. Each person has his own individual reaction to the change, and in addition a compounding effect results from the interaction of each employee with all the others. The outcome of a "simple" decision could result in an exponential calamity.

In order to successfully usher employees through the transition state, you need to constantly reinforce the future desired state and to allow for your employees' feelings, regardless of how irrational they may appear.

The future should be presented in three-dimensional Technicolor, yet the past should be respected. The ability to turn your back on the past and embrace the future is a function of reinforcement motivation. The vision for the future needs to be reinforced, underscored, highlighted, and celebrated. This needs to be done with discretion and strategy in order for people to "buy in" to the future vision.

The "buy in" process is essential for people to personally engage in the decision to change. Once they have chosen the change, have seen its validity, and are behind the effort, the major hurdles are out of the way. Management needs to be a living example of what it is espousing so that a credibility gap doesn't snowball into disillusionment. Once disillusionment sets in it can be overcome, but it creates a much bigger hurdle when added to the initial change project. Disillusionment is laden with multiple disappointments and hurts dating from the past, which are carried forward and compounded in the current situation.

The issues which seem to have the most intense charge, widespread impact, and are most difficult for people to deal with are:

♦ Abandonment, rejection, feeling unwanted, unloved, discarded, worthless.
♦ Disillusionment, disenchantment, disappointment, feeling lied to.
♦ Fear, lack of trust or faith, suspicion, anxiety, concern about integrity.
♦ Loss, separation, involuntary distancing, lack of connection.
♦ Control, loss of control and/or autonomy, powerlessness, issues with authority figures.

◆ Criticism, imperfections, feeling judged, inadequate, and/or unable.

◆ Dependence: relying on a parent or the organization to take care of needs.

◆ Responsibility: feeling responsible or to blame for outcomes.

◆ Boundaries: having porous or ambiguous boundaries.

◆ Authority issues: feeling a schism between self and authority figures.

◆ The need to be liked: having one's self-worth dependent on others' opinions.

When one of these issues is triggered in an individual, a whole chain of past events is frequently stimulated and brought to the present situation. These core issues make up the survival mechanism of each individual. When one of them gets triggered, the person's survival is threatened, and the reaction is subsequently disproportionate to the stimulus.

If you want to know if your company suffers from localized or interdepartmental negaholism, then take the following quiz.

IS YOUR COMPANY SUFFERING FROM INTERDEPARTMENTAL NEGAHOLISM?

1. Are individuals from one department, division, or subsidiary regularly talking about another work group in a snide, cynical, or sarcastic manner?

   YES ◇   NO ◇

2. Do the department heads avoid each other?

   YES ◇   NO ◇

3. Are some department heads engaged in unhealthy competition with each other?   YES ◇   NO ◇

4. Do different departments seem to have differing or conflicting goals?   YES ◇   NO ◇

5. Are conflicts between departments swept under the carpet because people are unable or unwilling to address the issues?   YES ◇   NO ◇

6. Is pertinent information or knowledge being withheld from a department that could benefit from having it?   YES ◇   NO ◇

7. Do departments seem to bicker and quarrel over trivial issues?   YES ◇   NO ◇

8. Do people in the departments compete rather than cooperate?   YES ◇   NO ◇

9. Is there a duplication of resources because of lack of cooperation?   YES ◇   NO ◇

10. Do the different work groups blame each other and point fingers regarding issues and concerns?   YES ◇   NO ◇

11. Is the relationship between work groups mostly antagonistic in nature?   YES ◇   NO ◇

12. Do you notice that there is inappropriate or guarded secrecy between work groups?   YES ◇   NO ◇

13. Do you observe an environment of mistrust between work groups?   YES ◇   NO ◇

14. Is there a lack of alignment between department heads, division heads, or managers?

YES ◇   NO ◇

15. Are there certain topics which should not be addressed in front of certain individuals from specific work groups?

YES ◇   NO ◇

16. Do employees from one work group think that another work group has only incompetent people working in it?

YES ◇   NO ◇

Do you observe that the department heads or managers are:

17. Motivated by means instead of ends?

YES ◇   NO ◇

18. Spending their time talking about the "other" work group?

YES ◇   NO ◇

19. Engaged in strategizing border skirmishes?

YES ◇   NO ◇

20. Focusing on winning their departmental battles and not on the big picture?

YES ◇   NO ◇

Do you notice people in those departments engaging in:

21. Secrecy?   YES ◇   NO ◇

22. Subterfuge?   YES ◇   NO ◇

23. Conspiracy?   YES ◇   NO ◇

24. Sabotage?   YES ◇   NO ◇

25. Undermining behavior?   YES ◇   NO ◇

26. Back-stabbing?   YES ◇   NO ◇

27. Setting people up for failure?   YES ◇   NO ◇

28. Collusion?   YES ◇   NO ◇

QUIZ SCORING

In order to determine the degree to which your departments are suffering from situational negaholism, score four points for every "YES" answer.

Now total your score and find your corporation on the scale below. If your score is:

0   Congratulate yourself on being part of a healthy, functioning organization where you can look forward to a productive and satisfying future.

1–30   This score denotes a mild case of situational negaholism. This environment, while not ideal, is functional and relatively healthy. If you take on a leadership role and become a change advocate, or better still, a change agent, you could be instrumental in helping the organization become even healthier. With a commitment to overcoming the dysfunctions, and with several (3–4) team-building sessions, you are well on the way to a fully functional future.

30–70   Your organization has strong tendencies towards situational negaholism. If you act now, you could clear up issues which might lead to a company-wide epidemic. Left unattended, they will grow into a chronic condition which will sooner or later affect the bottom line. A meeting of the department or division heads to discuss the situation would be the first step. The next step would be to diagnose the situation. Use the questionnaire to pinpoint the symptoms. If the condition is isolated to just two departments, a series of team-building sessions (5–8) should be effective. If the condition has spread to the consumer, you might well want to incorporate some customer satisfaction sessions with those employees who interface with the public directly. You can hire an organizational change agent/consultant to help you obtain an objective view.

70–120 You need to take your situation seriously. Without the proper measures, your organization is destined to become a certifiable negaholic corporation. Things have entered the danger zone, and active steps must be taken to rectify the situation. Things need to stabilize. You need to take this situation in hand and see how widespread it is. Start by giving this questionnaire to all the employees on an anonymous basis and assess your results. Start with a statement of purpose, a mission statement, and a list of goals and objectives. You need to get things back on track. You need to address the process of decision-making, leadership, values, structure, training, strategy, interpersonal dynamics, priorities, and organizational culture. You need to map out a master plan to address each issue and to ensure that all areas are covered in a methodical fashion.

CHAPTER 5

◆

IF IT AIN'T BROKE, DON'T FIX IT! WHAT DOES ''BROKE'' MEAN?

"If it ain't broke, don't fix it." This commonly-heard phrase rings through the halls of many traditional status quo–sustaining companies. The idea is to leave well enough alone. The question is: who decides what is broke, and what is well enough? Something may not be ''broke,'' but weakened and in need of fortification. Perhaps conditions in the marketplace have changed; what used to be effective no longer is, and may not even fulfill its original purpose.

Waiting for something to break before it is attended to is an old and costly behavior model. After the breaking point, it often takes more time and money to repair the damage than it would have if addressed earlier. After something has broken, the ''down'' time can be very costly and waste many people's time by preventing them from doing their jobs.

When a pain becomes severe enough, people and organizations take the necessary steps to stop it. When the pain is a minor inconvenience that doesn't impair function or can be tolerated, then no action is taken. However, when the fulfillment of an organization's purpose is threatened, and breakdowns in performance occur, then it is time to take the situation in hand and do something about it.

How do you determine when the pain is critical enough to stimulate you to action? When do you draw the line and say, "That's enough!"? Do conditions need to reach a fever pitch to motivate action? How do you assess the health of an organism when it is not in crisis? How do you anticipate and prevent a breakdown before it happens? These are critical questions that need to be addressed if organizational change is going to be effective.

The preventative model suggests that, given regular attention and periodic maintenance, breakdowns can be eliminated altogether. The idea is to have regular checkups, and pay to keep the organization healthy and in good running order. Most of us were taught that after a car is purchased, it needs to be serviced every three thousand miles or every three months. After the appropriate amount of time, the car goes into the shop for servicing. It gets a lube, oil, and filter, and everything else gets checked to ensure that it is in good running order. If the car needs a new fan belt, an alternator, a new battery, or new tires, you go ahead and anticipate the problem before it happens. It seems normal with cars. You wouldn't think of letting the car go until it gave out.

When you consider that an organization, which has many more moving parts than a car, will break down if left to its own devices, it sounds rather absurd to ignore regular check-ups. However, many organizations are expected to run on their own indefinitely, to fulfill their mission, and to produce results without any maintenance of the people who are its moving parts. By maintenance I mean the personal and interpersonal lube, oil, and filter, the quarterly or biannual servicing which examines everything *before* there is a problem.

Dick found himself in an interesting situation. He was the head of a successful division within a large publishing company. He felt that he shouldn't complain since there weren't any real problems. The division was, after all, producing well, meeting all commitments, and making a profit. Even though spirits weren't high, he felt he should be grateful that the division had maintained its market share for all these years while many other organizations had gone under. Not many other companies could claim that track record.

What was troubling Dick was a low-grade, non-specific malaise which was infecting two of his operating departments. Morale was low and people appeared apathetic, but they were turning out acceptable work. Dick was having conversations with himself. Part of him was willing to live with the situation. Things hadn't reached an intolerable point, and the pain wasn't so intense. He felt he could bear it. There was, however, another part of him which was dissatisfied and wanted things to change. His mental dialogue sounded like this:

"Things aren't right here," he muttered.

"Yeah, but this is the sixth largest company in the world," he rationalized.

"But people aren't happy," he retorted.

"Yeah, but the job's getting done; what are you complaining about?" he justified to himself.

"It's not fun to work here," he pouted.

"So now you want fun too? Why can't you be happy with success?"

"There's too much conflict between departments."

"So? There's been conflict between these departments since the beginning. Why are you getting upset now?"

"The work product is only average," he complained.

"What do you want? Sales are great, profits are good. Customers like our products, and you should too."

"I do like it. It's good. But it could be great, and that's what's bugging me. We have the ability to put out top-notch products, not just O.K. ones. I want us to strive for greatness."

"That's *your* problem. You're a perfectionist, and you'll never be satisfied. You're destined to be miserable. Couldn't you just relax and have a good time?" he countered.

"It's eating away at me, and it won't stop. I have to do something about it, at least for my own well-being," he protested.

"What are you, some kind of a nut? You've got a great job, people like you, and everything is going well. Why do you want to screw it up?" he reasoned.

"I've just got to do something about this situation. Maybe I'm crazy, but I want to find the joy I used to have; I want to want to come to work; I want to be happy doing my job," he argued.

"O.K., but I told you so. Don't blame me if it all blows up in your face."

Dick kept up these running dialogues with himself until he got tired, dismissed them, and got back to work. But every three days up popped the dialogue, and the same old refrain started all over again.

When I met Dick, he told me about his inner dia-

121

logue, and we set out on the journey to quiet the voices. I explained to him that two different parts of him were unaligned and were engaged in a conversation. In order to get the two parts aligned he had to make a choice. The alternatives were:

1. To keep the situation as it was and forget any ideas of change.
2. To change the present situation and make it different.
3. To set a future date to review the situation, and forget it for the moment.
4. To delegate the problem so that someone else would handle it.

I suggested that any one of the alternatives would be a viable solution, but what was critical was the *act* of choosing one.

Dick's main objective was to find again the desire to get out of bed in the morning. He didn't know what to do. After all, there wasn't any crisis, nothing was broken! There was just this nagging emptiness, a lack of joy, enthusiasm, and satisfaction.

After I gave a speech at Dick's company, we had a conversation about his situation. He asked me if I worked with companies to help establish goals and enable the key players to find their visions. I told him that I absolutely did that, and that the first step was to set up a meeting.

Several months later, I met with Dick and Dale—Dick's opposite in the sales department—for a full day. I first met with each of them individually and then with both of them together. They were more honest and direct than they had ever been with each other, and told each other things which they had thought but rarely, if ever, verbalized. It was a revelatory experience. They examined the future of the division with questions like: What was going to enable them to both retain their market share and simultaneously build new markets to expand their product line? What was going to breathe new life into the division without threatening its loyal customers? What was going to keep the staff engaged and vitally interested in a product which had run on a successful formula for decades?

These were hard questions to answer. Normally, if you have a successful product or service, you don't take a lot of risks, but rather do more of what you've already done in the past. If you know what works, don't change it, don't experiment, don't mess it up, just stay with what has worked before. These were the echoes in Dick's mind. There were two problems. First, what had worked in the past was not necessarily working in this changing marketplace. Second, it was mechanical and boring to do what had been done for six decades, and Dick and his colleagues wanted to be more innovative and creative.

The process of visioning assumes that you can envision, create, and conjure in your imagination. It assumes that you can picture what you would like rather than get caught up in what presently exists. The process of unlocking the door to your imagination is based upon the notion that everything that is created starts out with a single thought. The thought is a seedling which opens up the possibility of having things be different than they presently are. Walt Disney said, "If you can dream it, you can do it." Visioning invites the executive to dream beyond what is plausible and possible. Visioning enables you to take the leap into the unknown and create the desired future. Behind any accomplishment, significant or trivial, there exists a conscious or unconscious vision. The idea that people could go up in the sky and fly like birds was absurd until it worked. The notion of putting man on the moon was nothing more than an unrealistic dream until the day it actually happened. The dream of having the Berlin Wall come down was preposterous until the declaration was made. In companies, likewise, all major change starts with the seedling of a vision. Dick had begun the process of pursuing his dreams.

About a month had passed when Dick called to inquire about the next step. I said that a team-building session between the art department and the editorial staff sounded like the next logical step. He balked at the cost, and asked if there wasn't something simpler, shorter, and less expensive which could give him a taste of our work before his division committed to major culture change. I thought about it and suggested the Self Esteem/Inner Negotiation workshop, which is for people who have a glimmer of their vision and want to believe both in the vision and in their ability to make it happen. He said that it sounded appropriate, timely, and cost-effective, and immediately enrolled in the next workshop.

After Dick completed the Self Esteem/Inner Negotiation workshop, he was a believer. He believed that it was possible to make his dream come true, and he also believed that he had what it took to drive it home. He was also convinced that The MMS Institute could give him the help and guidance he wanted and needed in order to succeed. His vision was clearer and stronger than ever. He wasn't sure about the strategy or the method, but he knew, based upon what he had seen in the workshop, that something extraordinary could happen. He had begun to believe in possibility. He had seen enough to gamble, and he was ready to take the risk. We agreed to embark on a team-building project for his division.

I and my partner, Lynn Stewart, flew out to the Midwest to conduct our first set of meetings. We met with Dick and the three key executives who constituted the core group. We held separate interviews with each and asked questions like:

- What would you like to come out of the team-building project?
- What do you think are the issues which need to be addressed?
- What are your concerns about the project?
- What do you think might get in the way?

After the individual meetings, we met with all four executives together. It had become obvious in the individual meetings that some issues among the core group needed to be ironed out before we could expand and include the senior department heads. These issues included parameters of authority and responsibility, role clarification, trust, boundaries, respect, leadership, empowerment, and confusion about vision and direction. There were also discrepancies in individual management styles within the core group. These issues had to be addressed at this level before we could include the senior department heads.

If you asked one person about his perception of the company's direction, the answer you received wouldn't necessarily match with the next person's. There was confusion about the vision of the company, and frequently the staff didn't know which direction to take. It was unclear who to turn to for leadership.

Klaus, the group vice president, was the most indirect of all. Klaus didn't want to upset anybody, and therefore his style was to maintain the equilibrium, avoid ruffling feathers, and keep things on an even keel. Klaus wanted to keep things harmonious, so anything that was unpleasant was not to be discussed. Klaus was often hard to read, as well as mercurial. One day he would be obtuse and ambiguous, and the next day he would issue a mandate without conferring with anyone. People were confused by his ambiguity and perplexed by his inconsistencies.

Dick, who reported to Klaus, was a reluctant leader. He clearly had a leadership role, but he preferred to consult with his staff members rather than give them clear direction. He felt that the way to develop them was to encourage them to come up with their own solutions rather than having him tell them what he wanted. His subordinates, conversely, wanted clear direction from him. They wanted him to tell them what he wanted from them, what he wanted for the division, and what the company's direction, priorities, and future looked like.

Mia was Dick's operations manager. Where Dick had his eye on the big picture, Mia had hers on every step of the process. She was a very talented administrator and did an outstanding job, but her subordinates complained that she held the reins too tightly. They objected that she didn't allow them to create enough. They wished she were more like Dick in her style.

Then finally there was Chuck. Chuck was tough. He was a perfectionist who had never learned any tact. He didn't know how to give or receive criticism, complaints, or negative feedback. He would react to his department in the most volatile way. He would explode and then storm around huffing and puffing. His sense of product design was outstanding, but he had little to no people skills.

Those four—Klaus, Dick, Mia, and Chuck—comprised the core group. Their management styles spanned the broad spectrum. Employees noticed this and learned to scope out the situation and figure out who to go to when. The six department heads and their sixty or so staff members learned who would give them what they wanted. Just like children going to Mommy or Daddy, they knew who to turn to. If the subject were particularly touchy, they would approach Dick; if they wanted information and advice, they would seek out Mia. If they wanted to hear that everything would turn out fine, they would contact Klaus. But to a fault, at all costs, they would steer clear of Chuck.

In order to be successful in the team-building process, we had to start with the top, and facilitate some honest, direct communication before moving on to the other echelons. There was no way to deal with mixed messages between a manager and a subordinate if the issue hadn't been addressed between peers at the managerial level. If those issues were not resolved at the top, the result at any other level would be collusion between managers and their direct subordinates.

We all have weaknesses. Those weaknesses need to be addressed and strengthened, but the time and place in which they are discussed is critical. Interpersonal, managerial, organizational, and stylistic issues need to be attended to horizontally, one level at a time, before the vertical structure can be penetrated.

The purpose of the team-building project was to

build a cohesive team within the organization so that the environment felt like a close-knit family where co-workers combined efforts, in a spirit of cooperation, collaboration, and co-ownership, to accomplish the mission, goals, and objectives of the organization.

The project sounds easy, but in reality it is very challenging. People are complicated and need to be handled delicately. Reaching people at the behavioral, motivational, and emotional level is key in getting everyone to work together. Certain aspects of the employees' personalities need to be taken into consideration. Some of those aspects might be hidden agendas, past histories, old hurt feelings, political ambitions, concerns or fears about the future, discrepancies in management style, suspicions about each other, mistrust, and concerns about each other's competence.

The belief that you can't change people keeps the status quo in place. Often, people cling to their individuality and look at teamwork with disdain, which in itself contributes to discord, dissension, and disparity. In an organization comprised of highly creative people, individuality has a high value. Even the mention of the word "team" triggers fears about loss of identity. In managing change, the methodology of team-development is to work in concert with the persons affected by the change. This fosters responsibility in managers, which leads to creativity in problem resolution.

Each group has its own issues, and often they overlap. In order for people to feel safe, to begin to trust each other, and to venture out of their walled fortresses, they need to have structure and rules. These small group meetings were essential to laying a solid foundation upon which to build.

Mia wanted more definition and direction from

Dick. Dick wanted Chuck to calm down and ease up on the staff. Chuck wanted a new level of professionalism and excellence, and Klaus wanted everyone to be happy. Dick, Mia, and Chuck all agreed that Klaus was out of touch with reality and needed a dose of "what's really happening." Klaus felt strongly that Dick did not have enough direct hands-on contact with the division, and thought that too much had been delegated to Mia. Klaus also thought that Mia should take more of a back seat to Dick and not be so pushy. Mia did her job and minded her own business. As it was, they were all enormously competent individuals, but they were not a team. A team is two or more workers or players who put forth a concerted action or effort to achieve a common goal. This group was clearly not yet that.

Dick had come to believe that, collectively, they could really make the division what they wanted it to be. Klaus didn't see a need for the project, and wanted to leave well enough alone. Chuck was highly skeptical, and Mia was hopeful. They were in different worlds personally and professionally, and they had different expectations for the project.

Every now and again you have a chance of making the impossible happen, but only if everyone is committed to working together. However, the seeds of skepticism, cynicism, and doubt will not only inhibit the effort but kill the mission altogether. Pulling together a group of staunch individualists toward a common goal is no easy task. In the first place, it takes quality people who desire to become a team; second, it takes an enormous amount of willingness to go through the hoops and hurdles on the road to building a team; third, it takes commitment, the relentless tenacity to hang in there when the going gets rough.

Success in any team-development action rests on the fundamental belief that in an organizational setting the individual members must have the opportunity to grow if a vital organization is to remain healthy, or if an ailing one is to revive. The success of this project hinged on four key factors: the desire of the core group to effect the desired changes; its willingness to do whatever was needed to make it happen; its belief that it was possible to transform the corporate culture in this profound way; and its commitment to see the project through to the end.

Their individual stories were, as usual, very different, and formed a colorful mosaic when fitted together. Dick's story contributed to his being the reluctant leader. He remembered, "My father died when I was very young, and I was raised by my mother and my grandmother. They really wanted me to be happy. They must have felt guilty or something because I had no siblings or father, so they tried their best to do everything to make me happy. They would always ask me what I wanted. Of course, I didn't always know. Sure, I wanted ice cream and candy, but I didn't know important things like what I wanted to study, or where I wanted to camp, things like that. So they would work with me so that I could really find out what I liked, wanted, and what would make me happy. I felt like what I thought mattered to them. I guess that is where my values really started. I want the people who work for me to be really happy. I want them to enjoy their jobs and their lives just like my mother and grandmother wanted me to enjoy life. In my experience, people know what they want, and if given half the chance will tell you. You don't have to bully them around; they have the right instincts and will most often do the right thing."

Klaus came from a home with a very sick and abusive mother who literally drove him crazy. Conflict was so abhorrent to him that he did anything to avoid it. He was kind to everyone, but his kindness and his avoidance became entangled. He could not sort out the difference between caring about people and avoidance of reality.

Chuck was raised in a family marked by an absence of affection. He was emotionally neglected by both of his parents, and found that the only way he could get attention was by throwing tantrums. When he got angry, he was noticed. When he was happy, he was ignored. Unconsciously he formed the pattern of getting upset in order to be noticed. When he got the recognition that he needed, he saw that people were paying attention to him, which to him meant that he must be worth something.

Mia was raised in a home in which nobody ever did anything wrong. Hers was a perfect little family. She was expected to fit right in, and she did. She got straight A's in school and was the teacher's pet. She never got into trouble, and was so bright that it delighted all the adults in her world. She just wanted to go right along and be good, do good work, and have a nice day.

If you take a close look at these four personalities and their early childhood decisions, it is clear that all of them were doing the best they could given the information available to them. It is also apparent that their early experiences and decisions affected their adult attitudes, behaviors, and management styles. When you take these four people's different geographical backgrounds, couple that with their different beliefs, thoughts, feelings, and attitudes, and then on top of that superim-

131

pose their dysfunctional behavior patterns, you have to wonder at how remarkable it is that we got anything done at all.

After four meetings with the core group, it actually formed into a team. It was then time to bring the department heads on board. We met with each one of the six department heads. These interviews yielded the data which comprised our needs assessment. From the ten total interviews, we assembled a list of desired objectives for the team-building project. They were:

◆ To have a clear vision and sense of purpose as to where the publishing group is going. To have clear goals for the division that everyone has bought in to.

◆ To have a product that more fully addresses customers' needs and wishes. To generate excitement and satisfaction in customers. To get the spark back.

◆ To have an enhanced atmosphere of caring, respect, and appreciation for each other. To understand each other's eccentricities and moods. To work together as a group, to stop competing, and to build trust and honesty. To lessen defensiveness, turfiness, and backbiting.

◆ To better understand each department's problems and the company as a whole; to include people's feelings as well as the way the system runs. To perceive the division as a whole, not just as separate departments.

◆ To reduce stress, apprehension, and confusion on the job.

◆ To feel that we are making the world better in some way and that our contributions are recognized.

After the information was gathered, it was synthesized and fed back to the core group in a complete report. I asked the four executives if they were ready to embark on the journey toward resolving these issues and transforming the corporate culture. The group expressed doubt and concern, for it was not convinced that the issues were reconcilable.

"After all," said Dick, "the division has been this way for thirty years, ever since I've been here. Who's to say that it will ever be any different?"

I told them there was no guarantee that things would change, and that the most critical factor was their belief and commitment to having their work environment be the way they wanted it: safe, supportive, honest, direct, productive, and most of all, a fun and happy place to work. They were skeptical that they could individually or collectively make the changes which were required, but they were willing to trust our team-building experts.

Having midwifed change processes in the past, and having experienced the reactions of unprepared employees, I felt it was critical to explain the process and alert management to the various possible outcomes. After I completed my thorough briefing, they were well informed and chose to embark on the journey.

The whole project was a big risk. There was the potential that it would blow up in our faces. People could rebel and discredit the entire experience. The staff could collude, form a united front, and refuse to participate. On the other hand, employees could be apathetic, go along with the program in forced compliance, and agree with it even if it didn't work. The two extremes—rebellion or compliance—were unacceptable. The only acceptable outcome was communication, collaboration, and co-creation between the departments within the division. It was a hard line to hold, but the only desirable outcome was complete transformation.

In the series of meetings that followed, our objective was to make the shift from a dysfunctional culture to a functional one. We used our agreed-upon objectives as a measurement to determine progress.

It was difficult in the beginning, because people didn't know what to expect. They were reticent, fearful, and suspicious. They were unfamiliar with sitting down together, addressing differences, and working out a strategy which was mutually satisfying. Since the new behaviors were by definition alien, employees approached the tasks with nervousness and skepticism. They reminded me of people learning to ski for the first time: unused to slipping and sliding down the side of a mountain, their natural inclination was to dig in, hold on, and lean backward up the hill. All of their "natural" behaviors inhibited them from being successful at the new task at hand. In order to ski well, you have to physically move in ways that seem very unnatural to you. Unless you were taught to ski at a young age, you don't normally have your shoulders facing in one direction and your hips rotated ninety degrees in the opposite one. You have to make a shift from movements which are familiar, comfortable, and controllable to positions and moves which are strange, uncomfortable, and feel completely out of control.

The new movements that the division staff was learning were uncomfortable and unfamiliar. When the new behaviors became too awkward, the employees would tend to discuss the merits of their old ways of doing things and express the desire to revert to the past. After all, they were skilled in the old behaviors, and they were neophytes with the new ones. Who knew if these new ways of doing things would work anyway? Their old ways were good enough, and after all they had got them to where they were now. They couldn't be all that bad. They rationalized to keep themselves safe and secure. Most people, if given the choice, will choose familiar, predictable, and controllable behaviors, even if they are ineffective, rather than risk looking foolish or stupid and making blatant mistakes.

As we progressed, we used the orchestra as a team-building metaphor. In an orchestra, the conductor brings together a group of individualistic artists, and through communication, direction, and practice gets them to make music together. Harmonizing with each other, they don't lose their individuality, but rather create a more powerful and meaningful experience than they could ever create on their own.

Dick needed to become a conductor. Mia had to be prepared to be the concertmaster. Klaus was to be the patron of the arts who supported the effort, and Chuck was on the kettle drums in his own unique way. Rather than being separate entities, they had to come together and make music, which could only happen through the art of communication. Telling each other what they needed, what they wanted, what their challenges were, and rallying to support each other would all have to come from practice.

Very few of us were taught at home or at school how to work as a team. We weren't told to communicate when we felt we couldn't complete a task, or to reach out for support from each other. We were told to tell the truth, but we weren't encouraged to be really honest. We were told, "If you can't say something nice, don't say anything at all," which trained us to triangle com-

135

munication and go to a third party to address unpleasant situations. Most of us were schooled to avoid conflict and to be nice people rather than to deal with the real truth of a situation. Many of us learned that it was natural to defend our ideas, and that if others disagreed it was appropriate to attack theirs. Discussing how we felt about situations and projects was definitely not part of the agenda, and acting as if we had it all together and could do anything was standard operating procedure. Perhaps we were told, "Don't think you're so great, you'll get a swelled head," an admonition meant to imprint on us such behaviors as being modest, not tooting our own horn, and appearing humble.

The project at first addressed contextual issues like direction, mission, purpose, and objectives for the division in general. The next level focused on the main issues which were preventing employees from functioning effectively as a team. Additionally, it became clear that we needed to teach some real communication techniques which would be fundamentally important in individual as well as group meetings.

The project lasted for nine months, and was similar to other team-building projects in that it had its own life cycle. It started out with enthusiasm amid some skepticism. Around May the entire project almost aborted, since people's frames of reference were dramatically threatened. One actually wrote me an anonymous note which said:

There is an increased sense of powerlessness on the part of the staff, because CLEARLY—major issues are not being resolved. Why? Because management is not LISTENING, not HEARING what we are saying, despite sincere intent, and some members of the management team continue to respond in the same arrogant, me-me-me, controlling and defensive (turfy) way that created many of our morale problems in the first place. The responsible parties— seem unable or unwilling to dispassionately HEAR what the staff is trying to say.

These issues are not unique to this client. Frequently, employees sound like children who cry out, "See me, hear me, listen to me, and notice me. I have needs and wants, please recognize me, and take what I'm saying seriously." I hear concerns such as these frequently from clients. If you don't have the skills to effectively deal with upset or dissatisfied customers or employees, then when dissatisfaction becomes an issue, you will want to play ostrich, bury your head in paperwork, and ignore their demands.

In our team-building sessions, we put the issues on the table. We started by tackling the items head-on, one at a time, issues like arbitrary changes, choosing alternatives which Dick didn't agree with, and making decisions without conferring with your counterpart. We addressed issues like hurt feelings which were a result of miscommunication, lack of communication, or no communication at all. We discussed heretofore unconfrontable issues.

There were times when no one was willing to speak. The air was thick with tension, and a coin flip would determine whether the best alternative to alleviating it was cracking a joke or leaving the room. People did not want to be responsible for initiating discussion of the taboo topic. Why couldn't they speak? What was so unspeakable? What would draw such a reaction that it wasn't worth the risk?

Finally Bart said, "I think we're all afraid to talk. We're afraid of pointing the finger. We're scared to be the one to open up the discussion and risk the disapproval of the others."

Then Katie jumped in, "I think we're afraid to say anything mean. We're all such nice people here, we don't want to dispel the myth. If we don't bring up the skeletons then we can pretend that everything is just fine. The truth is things aren't fine, and we don't want to admit it."

Sally stopped holding back. "All right, I'll say it if nobody else will. We think management is against us, and we talk about how to beat it at its own game all the time. We spend a lot of time planning on how to retaliate and win the game. We think that you try to make life difficult for us, and that we have to protect ourselves against your undermining our efforts."

Sally burst out with, "It's just like what happened between Gene and me."

I asked what happened.

"Oh, nothing really," she said, embarrassed.

"Either we're going to talk about these situations, or let's go back to our jobs and call it a day. Someone has to be brave here and take a risk or we're never going to get anywhere. Sally, will you be the one?" I invited.

"Well it's really stupid, and he knows what I'm talking about," she said defensively.

"I don't have a clue what you're talking about," Gene countered.

"You do too. It was that report on the new product line. You sabotaged me and you know it," Sally said vehemently.

"I don't know what she's talking about," Gene said in a dismissive tone.

I had to intervene at this point: "I want to reinforce the rules for team-building. They are posted on the wall, but the specific ones which I want to remind you of are: no interrupting, no attacking and no defending. I can only facilitate this process if we abide by the rules and play fair. Sally, would you care to tell the story from your point of view? When you're done, then we'll hear from Gene."

"I was writing a report on the sales potential of our newest line of titles. I had conducted dozens of interviews with customers, both in person and over the phone, and had dedicated a lot of my time and energy to the project. I was really happy with the way the report turned out, and then he ruined it," she said emphatically.

"Please leave out the accusations," I implored. "First tell what happened, and then we'll address your feelings about the situation. I know that you're upset, but I want to eliminate the attack/defend mode and see if we can dissect the situation together to find out what really happened."

"O.K. Things were really rushed; there wasn't time to sit down and have a meeting. He called me on the phone and said there wasn't enough time to run the computer research I had asked for, but he could give me some old data he already had. I said I didn't like the idea, and he said he was sorry, but that was the best he could do," Sally said with resentment. "Then the report got published with the old data that didn't support my telephone research. All my work was ruined," she said, on the verge of tears.

"Thanks, Sally. I know that this was a difficult and painful story to recount. I want to thank you for talking about it in front of all of us. I know it was hard, and you were very brave to do it. Gene, will you tell us what happened from your point of view?" I inquired.

"Sure, but it was really different for me," Gene said, shaking his head.

"That's O.K., that's usually the case," I said.

"I kept asking what research she wanted, over and over again, and she kept delaying. I asked her for it four times while I had the time to work on it. When I finally got her request, it was too late. I was working on three other projects and I didn't have the time to devote to her research. I was rushed and did the best I could, given the time restraints. Hers isn't the only project I have to work on. Given the time-frames that we agreed upon, I could have given her a lot more attention, but since she was so late, I just couldn't," Gene said candidly.

"It sounds like time pressures and a breakdown in communication were at the root of this unfortunate circumstance," I said with certainty. "I also hear some hurt feelings, and many assumptions. Let's take it one step further. Gene, how did you feel when Sally didn't get you the research request when it was promised?"

"I felt frustrated the first time, but figured she knew what she was doing. When I kept getting put off, though, I started really getting mad," he said.

"What else, Gene?" I asked.

"I felt like she thinks I can just pull rabbits out of hats and jump through hoops for her. I thought to myself, why, she doesn't care if I end up staying up all night doing the research for her report, she doesn't show me any consideration at all. She treats me like a lackey, like I work for her. She thinks I'm supposed to be at her beck and call. It's as if I've got nothing better to do than punch my damn computer even when she's three weeks late," Gene said.

"Sally, what were your feelings in this situation?" I asked.

"I felt rushed, of course. I also felt pressured to get it done. When Gene kept asking for the research request, it only intensified the pressure. When I got the request to him I felt relieved, but I also felt a lot of guilt. He seemed distant towards me, and I was proud of the report, but I couldn't even get excited because of all the guilt I felt for being so late," Sally said honestly.

"What else, Sally? What about when you saw the published report? What did you feel then?"

"I was furious. I was shocked that he had inserted the old data. I felt disregarded, discounted, and discarded. I felt so small. It was like I was working for him. All my work had gone down the drain, and I felt so unimportant. It was awful. I was ashamed and hurt. As a result, I haven't talked to him since that incident," she said with a quiver in her voice.

"It sounds like there were hurt feelings on both sides of this situation. Big misunderstandings and virtually no communication created this massive breakdown. Is there any way to heal this situation?" I inquired.

"I guess I want to say, for my part, that I'm sorry," Gene said sympathetically. "I never meant to upset you like this. I can understand your feelings and I'm really sorry to have caused you this pain."

"I guess I should have called you and told you what was happening with the request, and asked you read the rough copy of the report to see if you were seeing it the way that I was. I could have included you in the decision-making process, rather than excluding you and then expecting so much from you at the very end. I'm sorry for operating so autonomously. I wonder if we can ever change," Sally said thoughtfully.

141

"What is important here is to discover what each one of us did, not to point the finger, but to learn something about our own behavior, to see what we should do differently next time, and to set out to change our behaviors for the future," I said.

After that, we listed everything that could be learned from the situation on a flip chart in order to extrapolate universal lessons which could be applied to many other situations.

After several conversations with Sally, it became evident that she had learned her behaviors in childhood. When she had asked questions, her mother said, "You ask too many questions! If you just give it some thought, I bet you can figure it out on your own." She learned to stop asking questions and to figure things out on her own. She put a lid on her innate inquisitiveness, and started to second-guess people's behaviors, motives, and wishes.

Gene had been the only child in a family where both parents worked. He was talented and received much attention for his artistic ability. He spent hours working by himself and paying close attention to his drawings and paintings. He was a fairly introverted person and was content to work on his own. Throughout his childhood Gene felt pressures to be something or do something, but for the life of him he didn't know what.

Interestingly enough, Sally's pattern of not asking questions dovetailed nicely with Gene's tendencies toward solitude. She assumed and conjectured, and he avoided. Neither had the communication or interpersonal skills to bridge the gap. Neither ventured out, and the gap only widened.

The situation between Sally and Gene was only

one example of the different ways people operate and how those differences cause tension. Instead of assuming, conjecturing, and projecting, they could have discussed their expectations, reviewed their assumptions, and explored their feelings about the situation. Rather than second-guessing, they could have simply asked direct questions. Rather than waiting to see if things would work out, they could have addressed their concerns and fears early on so that they could plan an alternate strategy which would avoid a collision course.

In the end, they had a dramatic breakthrough. They set their objectives, and were tenacious in going for everything they wanted. Their success didn't mean that no more work was required, but certainly that with maintenance all things were possible. They had the courage to envision a new and different future, to break old patterns of behavior, and to believe they could create a truly magical work environment. They really made it happen.

Team development of this type reflects two aspects of organizational development. They are:

♦ managing change.
♦ focusing human energy toward specific desired outcomes.

Team development is practical and functions as a discipline for focusing energy on specific goals. While most organizations begin purposefully, the goals of groups give way to individualistic aims. Team development recognizes that all energy must be volunteered by individual managers. The wants and needs of the individual are therefore essential to the goal-setting process of the group. If each member participates in forming group goals and in general subscribes to those goals, then a considerable share of his or her energy and the energy of co-workers begins to work toward a common purpose. This type of organization exhibits independence, optimism, interdependence, and a high degree of responsibility and achievement.

In managing change, the methodology of team development is to work in concert with the persons affected by the change. This fosters responsibility in managers, which leads to creativity in problem resolution. What is true of individuals then becomes true of the associations they form.

Team development actions succeed when leaders proceed by:

- ◆ Working with managers affected by changes in an organization.
- ◆ Forming ties with all those who can influence desired outcomes.
- ◆ Identifying and forming tentative basic goals, which by general agreement will be converted into specific group goals.
- ◆ Changing the environment from one in which managers are conditioned to interpersonal conflict (I-you) to one in which collaboration and healthy competition (we) is the rule. To bring about such a change, open communication, collaborative goal-setting, and mutual problem-solving/decision-making must be encouraged.
- ◆ Building active feedback loops so that managers monitor and share in their organization's progress .toward the achievement of mutually agreed-upon goals.

144

The final outcome of the group's efforts, nine months later, was triumphant. All of its objectives were achieved, and it had grown into a confident team that felt empowered by its own success. We, the consultants, instructed, coached, and supported them throughout the process. We wouldn't let them give up when things got uncomfortable. One member of the group sent us a final letter:

Our intensive monthly sessions this last year have produced results far beyond anything I would have ever expected from such a program. You have helped us cure dysfunctional behavior that has persisted for as long as the thirty years I've been in this company!

There's been a general uplifting of staff morale, and a couple of outstanding cases of staffers who have been changed from problem employees into cheerful, super producers. We've all become more honest with each other and have learned to deal openly and effectively with conflict.

I watched an exchange among three staff people in a meeting the other day which would have made you proud. A serious disagreement was aired by a person who, a year ago, would never have spoken out. The two other people in the discussion handled it without rancor and a compromise was worked out in minutes with no hard feelings. Best of all, they did it with no intervention from me.

A healthy organization is one that has a strong sense of its own identity and mission, plus the capacity to adapt readily and constructively to change. This type of organization exhibits independence, optimism, an ability to share responsibility, and great results. Even today, several years later, the employees say the results are permanent because they came up with their own solutions—they implemented the changes, and they owned the results.

PART III

◇

THE NEGAHOLIC
CORPORATION

CHAPTER 6

◆

WHAT IS
A NEGAHOLIC
CORPORATION?

Do you ever notice that you or the people in your work environment:

◆ Say "Yes" when they really mean "No" because they are afraid of saying the wrong thing, hurting someone's feelings, causing a problem, or are certain that saying "No" is just not an option?
◆ Ignore situations which are untenable because they don't know what to do about them, are afraid of alienating someone, or are scared of losing their jobs?
◆ Are confused about the direction, the strategy, the priorities, or even the purpose of the business?
◆ Work to please someone higher up rather than because of an inner sense of satisfaction?
◆ Gossip, lobby, and collude with each other rather than address the problem at hand?

149

- Focus on protecting themselves and maintaining a low profile rather than speaking up to a person who can effect a change?
- Undermine, back-stab, or sabotage their co-workers rather than operate as a team?
- Wish things will change, hope that something or someone will save the day and make everything all better, or live with a fantasy of better things to come?
- Are resigned that things will never change, and feel the best they can do is get through the day and collect a paycheck?

If you answered "Yes" to any of these questions, then chances are you work in a negaholic corporation and may even be a negaholic worker yourself.

If you cannot differentiate your organizational culture from the dysfunctional behaviors of the individuals in it, you and your company are suffering from corporate negaholism.

HOW DOES IT START?

Corporate negaholism has many sources. For example, it can come directly from a founder who carries the negaholic virus when he starts his own organization. He may bring his own personal dysfunctions to the corporation and cause the organization to be systemically unhealthy from its inception.

Fred, an entrepreneurial type with an excess of enthusiasm, decided to leave his career as an attorney and start his own bicycle shop. He was tired of working in a large law firm. He was frustrated with the bureaucracy, and wanted to use his hands as well as his head. Fred was so excited about his dream coming true that he forgot to have an entrepreneurial check-up. He overlooked determining whether he had all the essential pieces in place in order for the business to succeed. He was strong on finding a good location, re-searching the market, and financing the enterprise. He was efficient at ordering the product, meeting his deadlines, and hiring a staff which reflected his per-sonable demeanor.

Fred forgot one thing: financial management. He was dreadful with numbers, had barely squeaked through third-year math, and hated bookkeeping. Fred had not thought about who would keep track of cash flow. His enthusiasm obscured the reality of bean-counting.

Fred came from a fairly well-off family and never had to worry about finances. When he needed money, he asked for it and got it. It was that simple. He never had to balance his checkbook, nor did he have to ac-count to anyone for how much money he spent.

This wasn't an issue in the large law firm, but left to his own devices, Fred was up against a bigger challenge than he knew. He could no longer act as if he had un-limited funds, nor could he hope that his lack of ac-countability would be absorbed by a large firm. He had chosen to go it alone, and along with the thrill of risk-taking, he had to deal with the reality of his strengths and weaknesses.

When he started the business, he was confident. He knew that, with his natural abilities and his charm, he could sell ice to Eskimos. Fred was right. He was well aware of his strengths and he used them well. The busi-ness flourished; it was an overnight success, and Fred was flying. Each month he doubled his gross, until after a year taxes were due. Fred called Jay, an old school chum who was a CPA. He asked Jay if he would do his taxes, and Jay willingly agreed.

When Jay saw the condition of Fred's finances, he was appalled. There were deposits and checks made out to himself with no explanation. There was no general ledger, and inventory control was nonexistent. There were missing checks, missing deposit slips, and loan histories were unheard of.

Fred had never put a priority on financial management, and now he had to pay the price. Even though he disliked it, he had to sit down with Jay and try to unscramble the puzzle which he had created. After many painstaking hours of work and hundreds of questions, they unscrambled and sorted out the pieces of Fred's financial history. It cost Fred a fair amount to the IRS, but he learned an important lesson and the business was saved. Fred ultimately opened up several more bike shops and was very successful. His dysfunction was his avoidance and denial of his weaknesses.

Since he was the only son of an older couple who had wanted to have a child for many years, Fred was doted upon and worshipped by both his parents. His mother especially couldn't bear for anyone to say an unkind word about her darling Freddy. He was the pinnacle of perfection, the apple of her eye, and could do no wrong. When he didn't do well in school, she would blame the teachers and say that they hadn't prepared the children well enough for the exam. When he had romantic difficulties, she would blame the girls and say that they simply weren't good enough for him. When he didn't do well in sports, she would say that the team needed a new coach who understood the boys better. She protected Fred from disappointment and all negative feelings by shielding him from all personal responsibility.

Luckily, Fred didn't grow up to be a complete monster. He did, however, formulate a critical dysfunction: the inability to admit and deal with the weaknesses within himself. His lack of financial management skills was a concern since he needed these skills in his new venture. But skills can be learned; a more serious concern was his blindness to his own foibles. As a result of a crisis, and with the support of his friend Jay, Fred finally faced his personal dysfunction, overcame his weakness in math, and saved his business before it was too late. This systemic type of negaholism can occur in entrepreneurial companies, privately-held companies, or in corporations both private and public.

MERGING WITH THE NEGAHOLIC VIRUS

If you are in an organization, there are two main ways the virus can infect the corporation: through mergers with unhealthy or negaholic corporations, or through the acquisition of unhealthy firms. If the dysfunction is not addressed, then after direct contact the healthy organization becomes infected, and the contagion begins to spread.

Carl, the owner of a chain of successful small fast-food restaurants, decided to merge with a multinational restaurant chain which had a wealth of capital to invest in developing his chain. It looked like a great opportunity all the way around. The restaurant concept was firmly in place, the quality of the food, the service, and the ambiance in all of the five restaurants were consistently high. Carl was proud of what he had accomplished. After an outside audit and an examination of the alternatives, Carl decided that a merger was the answer. After all, he could continue his dream business, have a lot more money in the corporate checkbook, and quadruple the stakes overnight. It looked perfect!

After the merger, the new key executives came into the business with complete disregard for its culture. Dick and Jim began throwing their weight around, changing policies, calling meetings with miscellaneous personnel, and doing whatever suited them whenever they pleased. They devalued human resources, a respected department in the company. They declared that from now on no money would be spent in training or HR. They ended participative management and initiated an authoritarian style of management. People were treated as objects, pawns in the grand game of making money.

Carl was beside himself. His healthy company was infected with the "Theory X" strain of negaholic virus. Theory X, a term coined by Douglas McGregor, embodies three usually unconscious assumptions about people and their relationship to work. The assumptions are: people don't like to work and will avoid it if they can; most people must be coerced, controlled, directed, or threatened with punishment to get them to exert any effort toward the achievement or organizational objectives; and the average person prefers to be directed, wishes to avoid responsibility, has relatively little ambition, and wants security above all else. The contamination of the Theory X virus was spreading with each contact. Previously productive, happy employees were turning into withdrawn, resentful, and even openly rebellious dissenters. The term "team" was replaced by "staff," and people began to feel their caring and nurturing environment turn into a cold and dehumanized one.

Carl had a decision to make. Should he try to raise the money to buy out Dick and Jim? Should he just go along with their program? Or should he figure out a way for Dick and Jim to buy him out? The decision was a tough one. This company had been his baby. He had invested time, energy, and money over the last five years in the concept, development, and creation of his dream restaurant. He knew that to make a restaurant successful several ingredients were essential. An ideal location was vital, as was really good food. If you wanted to succeed over the long term, then you had to have a great group of employees who really liked people, and who delighted in giving them the care and attention necessary to make their dining experience extraordinary. It was also equally important to provide a work environment which was supportive of the overall restaurant concept.

Carl had done his homework, put in his time and commitment, and accomplished the desired result. He had labored day and night for five years, not including his time at all the restaurants he had worked in prior to owning his own, and now he was about to lose it all. He wrestled with the decision, and vacillated many times. "Maybe it *can* work," Carl thought to himself. "These guys aren't all that bad. Lots of different types of people work together. We can find a way. The beginning of anything is always tough. This is just the initial getting-to-know-you phase, and we're all uneasy. Maybe they'll calm down in a while." Carl reconsidered his intentions of selling out.

Then Jim would do something unpleasant, like

emptying an employee's desk out onto the floor in the hallway without conferring with her, and Carl would think: "I've got to get out. I can't stand coming in to work. It's driving me crazy watching the way he treats the Team. It hurts me to see my employees so diminished and devalued. It sounds like chalk on a blackboard every time he yells at someone. I can't take it anymore." Carl would allow himself to feel the pain of watching his precious and treasured labors destroyed before his very eyes.

He would muse: "I'm sure I can raise the money and buy these guys out. We have lots of investors who care about the business and will come up with the bucks. I can't leave now. I can't walk out on those people who believed in me and are here because of me. Where is my loyalty, my sense of commitment? There has got to be another way!" Carl felt the pangs of his moral obligation.

Then he would reconsider: "But what about my investment? Would I come out all right by walking away? Wouldn't I do much better by sticking around? In the next two years, we could open twenty restaurants. I'll miss out on reaping the rewards. In two years we could go public and that's what I've been waiting for. I can't leave now, we're on the brink of the big time. I better see if I can reason with these guys." Carl would think logically and be mindful of his investment.

So it went, and Carl simply could not come to a decision. Month after month passed as he continued to consider his options. Carl was resorting to his familiar dysfunction, procrastination, and avoiding his obligations.

Finally, he decided to raise the money and buy out the investors. It was going to be a challenge, and he was nervous about the risks involved, but he felt he couldn't abandon all the work he had put into the business. He met with investors one by one, addressed their concerns and considerations, and recruited their financial backing. Together with an army of loyal and trusting supporters, he bought back the company and chose to reclaim his creation. He was proud that he went for the long haul and didn't abandon his dream. Carl felt happy he had taken the risk, trusted himself, and won.

NEGAHOLIC ACQUIRERS

A third way that companies become negaholic is through being acquired by an unhealthy company. The following story illustrates how a healthy company taken over by a negaholic company can ultimately be destroyed.

One of the top firms in the entertainment industry was interested in acquiring a computer component manufacturing company. The CEO of the small computer firm was a Taiwanese man, Chen, who was gentle, mild-mannered, and very loving toward his employees. The culture was harmonious and peaceful. The environment was so placid that you could picture a group of employees doing t'ai chi during lunchtime. He ran his operation as if it were a small, tightly-knit family unit. People enjoyed working there, and everything flowed smoothly. The majority of the employees were Taiwanese women who spoke limited English. Chen, noting their need to improve their language skills, provided English classes for the staff. Rarely was a harsh word uttered, and concern for the well-being of everyone abounded.

The large conglomerate was eager to pursue the acquisition of Chen's company, and as all the numbers fit into the grand scheme of things and the transaction looked good on paper, it decided to proceed. The primary motivation for the transaction was to place the inventor of the laser disk, which was on the cutting edge of the new technology, at the head of this small computer company; the inventor could thus have a greenhouse-like environment in which to conduct his research and development of the new product. Everything seemed to be progressing well: the inventor and Chen were very compatible, and there was peace in the valley.

When the employees were told about the upcoming acquisition by the larger company, they were excited. It sounded as if the small happy family would grow into a large happy family. The idea of meeting their new corporate brothers and sisters was heartwarming. The office was buzzing with activity and excitement. The big and powerful company that was going to acquire them offered many new opportunities. Things could only get better, they thought.

Members of the conglomerate visited the small computer firm. Notes were taken, observations were made, and then they left. The corporate decision-makers were assessing what changes needed to be made in terms of the new acquisition. The large conglomerate decided that the peaceful culture of the small computer company was incompatible with its own; it needed to be integrated into the more frenetic pace of the larger company. Birthday parties in the office, celebrating Taiwanese holidays, and singing Tai songs in the late afternoon were considered unprofessional and hokey by the megacompany. The team in charge of acquisitions decided that it had to clamp down. Some decisions had to be made which would tighten things up and make the outfit more professional. Suddenly, as if overnight, age-old privileges were revoked, rules were posted, lengthy reports were required, and complicated bureaucratic mandates prevailed.

The inventor, who was seeking a cloistered environment in which to create, was promoted to general manager, and Chen was removed. All English classes were abolished, and communication was handled through memos posted in English. The employees literally didn't know what had hit them. They felt as if a bomb had been dropped on their tranquil little office. Chaos ruled. Not only was communication sporadic and incomplete, but it also was not translated into their native tongue. With its leader, Chen, gone, and the inventor—who was not a leader at all, didn't speak their language, and only wanted to do research and development—at the helm, the little company took a nosedive. Morale deteriorated, people stopped talking to each other, and teamwork declined. People were confused and didn't understand what was happening. They felt embarrassed at not understanding what was happening and didn't know who to turn to. Productivity plummeted, and the fabric of the organization unraveled rapidly.

The final outcome of the acquisition was that the small computer company fell apart, and eventually appeared on the books as a $250,000 write-off. The inventor and his laser disk project were sold to another major entertainment conglomerate, which used the opportunity to corner the market and become the leader in laser disk technology. The rest of the Taiwanese employees scattered in search of fair havens and more tranquil waters.

NEGAHOLIC ACQUISITIONS

The negaholic virus can spread in two ways. The last two examples were of how a healthy company can be acquired by a negaholic one. The other type of situation is the reverse of that: a healthy company can acquire a negaholic one.

A full-service financial consulting firm was acquiring another financial consulting firm. The firm being acquired was producing over $10 million in gross revenues per year. The revenues doubled every year, and the business seemed to be flourishing. After about twenty years thousands of clients were on the books, and the seemingly healthy business was ripe for sale. During the previous twenty years, Allan, the founder/ owner, had put together hundreds of partnerships, most of them in real estate and trusts, as well as having underwritten $55 million worth of loans.

When it came time to finalize the paperwork concerning the buy-out, many unsuspected skeletons started creeping out of the closet. One of the skeletons was that Allan had written a letter to all of his clients stating that the firm would make up all of their losses. In other words, the financial consulting firm had formed partnerships with individuals to invest in a myriad of opportunities. Allan also volunteered to take back all of the partnerships which hadn't worked out. The purchasing company now realized that it would be paying out $16,000 per month on the old partnerships, and that it would cost between $1 million to $2 million per year to pay off the old debt. The deal was still alive, but this new information was an eye-opener, and changed the negotiation tactics accordingly. Steve, the CEO of the acquiring firm, had to make his conditions for purchasing clear. He had to ensure that there was an opportunity to win the game if his company were to buy Allan's company. The negotiations were acceptable on both sides, and Steve had his work cut out for him. He had to make some drastic changes in order to weed out the old virus mentality and turn the situation into a healthy one.

One of the changes which had to take place in Allan's company was a shift from a lavish country club mentality where spending was no issue to a new regime where budgets, targets, and marketing strategies were the primary focus. The tighten-your-belt strategy made some people very edgy. Rumors flew like a swarm of bees throughout the organization. People were speculating on whether the company would be around next month or even next week. Employees kept comparing the new style of management with the good old days, and muttering their dissatisfaction with the present situation. Nostalgia was rampant, résumé comparisons dominated coffee breaks, and employees were handing in their resignations in gloomy anticipation of being let go. The spirit that once filled the sails of the company seemed to have died.

The healthy company which was buying Allan's realized that it had to embark upon a whole new strategy with respect to the negaholic-infested firm. It approached the acquired company as if it had termites; whatever parts were eaten away had to be let go, and whatever parts were salvageable would be saved. It wanted to allow the old culture to die, and breathe life into what was healthy. Steve knew the magnitude of the task and was reticent, but marched into the fray.

Steve was operating from three main assumptions: people want to win, they want to be productive, and they want to be included. All of his actions stemmed from these three basic premises. He created a brilliant vision of the future with the participation of those who were on board for the long haul. The vision: "To change how every person on the planet interacts with economics so that everyone has the opportunity to operate from choice." He reinforced this vision to the acquired company in every way imaginable. He had it posted where everyone could see it. It would be stated in company meetings. There was a new organization chart which spelled out clear expectations and new lines of communication. The compensation plan was totally revamped so that it was fair and reasonable.

At the end of every week, meetings were now held in which people had to state their successes and accomplishments over the last five days. If employees had difficulties, their co-workers were encouraged to remind them of their wins for the week. There were a lot of verbal pats on the back, and a new benefit plan, including a profit-sharing plan, was developed which would enable employees to literally own part of the company. Steve also made a major commitment to stamping out gossip. Dysfunctional behavior was brought out into the open and dealt with supportively and openly. The turn-around strategy was to reinforce what the acquiring firm wanted more of and to minimize what it wanted to diminish.

In this situation, the negaholic growth was isolated and weeded out before contamination could occur. Fortunately, Steve and the people in the acquiring firm were functional and healthy enough to spot the signs of negaholism and to take action before contagion spread to the parent company. All too often, companies are blind to the subtle nature of negaholism, and because of their own avoidance and denial overlook what is staring them right in the face.

One or all of these scenarios may sound familiar to you. To determine whether or not your own company is systemically negaholic, take the following quiz. This is not an ordinary quiz, but rather a corporate assessment tool which will determine to what degree your company is afflicted with corporate negaholism. In the next five minutes you will know how serious the situation is.

ARE YOU A PART OF A NEGAHOLIC CORPORATION?

1. Are feelings in your workplace often avoided, discounted, suppressed, or denied?   YES ◇   NO ◇

2. Do you feel that your thoughts, comments, and feedback are ignored, not taken seriously, and that what you have to say isn't valued?   YES ◇   NO ◇

3. Is there an unspoken contact about maintaining the status quo, even if policies, practices, and the direction of the company are inappropriate, unethical, or wrong?   YES ◇   NO ◇

4. Do you find the direction of the company changing without sufficient research, planning, or notice?   YES ◇   NO ◇

163

5. Are root issues swept under the carpet because people are unable or unwilling to address them with the people who possess the authority to effect a result? YES ◇ NO ◇

6. Do you observe people colluding with each other rather than confronting the person with whom they are taking issue? YES ◇ NO ◇

7. Do you see the decision-making process as inconsistent, erratic, or unpredictable? YES ◇ NO ◇

8. Does the environment espouse one standard and in practice operate in a radically different manner? YES ◇ NO ◇

9. Does the environment encourage people to become consumed by their jobs to the detriment of their personal lives? YES ◇ NO ◇

10. Does the environment promote workaholism as a corollary to recognition and getting ahead? YES ◇ NO ◇

11. Do you observe people denying the existence of particular situations because they are unable to deal with them (i.e., drug use, drinking, fraternization on the job, cheating, stealing, misappropriation of funds, or unethical behavior)? YES ◇ NO ◇

12. Do you find that employees are unable or unwilling to confront inequities, untruths, or broken agreements? YES ◇ NO ◇

13. Do you observe people clinging to their old ways of doing things, and building alliances geared toward blocking the changes which have been mandated?

    YES ◇   NO ◇

14. Do you notice that there are secrets which are guarded and protected by those whose loyalty to the corporation is paramount?   YES ◇   NO ◇

15. Do fear and mistrust permeate the environment?

    YES ◇   NO ◇

16. Is there misalignment between the chief executive, the directors, and/or the managers regarding priorities, objectives, and direction?   YES ◇   NO ◇

17. Are unproductive people neglected rather than having their problems addressed directly?

    YES ◇   NO ◇

Are the key executives:

18. Ineffective?   YES ◇   NO ◇

19. Moody?   YES ◇   NO ◇

20. Compulsive?   YES ◇   NO ◇

21. Paranoid?   YES ◇   NO ◇

22. Repressive?   YES ◇   NO ◇

23. Overly controlling?   YES ◇   NO ◇

24. Depressed?   YES ◇   NO ◇

25. Following the directives and orders blindly, without questioning their impact on the health and well-being of the organization or its members?

                                                                       YES ◇   NO ◇

26. Spending too much or too little money?

                                                                       YES ◇   NO ◇

27. Eating too much?   YES ◇   NO ◇

28. Drinking too much?   YES ◇   NO ◇

29. Inconsistent and/or abusive in their management style?   YES ◇   NO ◇

30. Excessively friendly with the opposite sex on the job?   YES ◇   NO ◇

31. Working themselves to exhaustion? YES ◇   NO ◇

32. Having frequent outbursts in the office and using other people to excuse or explain their behavior?

                                                                       YES ◇   NO ◇

Are the people around you frequently:

33. Frustrated?   YES ◇   NO ◇

34. Anxious?   YES ◇   NO ◇

35. Confused?　　　　　　　　YES ◇　　NO ◇

36. Depressed?　　　　　　　　YES ◇　　NO ◇

37. Angry?　　　　　　　　　　YES ◇　　NO ◇

38. Timid?　　　　　　　　　　YES ◇　　NO ◇

39. Fearful?　　　　　　　　　YES ◇　　NO ◇

40. Afraid of making mistakes and losing their jobs?
　　　　　　　　　　　　　　YES ◇　　NO ◇

41. Resigned that things will never change?
　　　　　　　　　　　　　　YES ◇　　NO ◇

42. TGIF: living for Friday?　　YES ◇　　NO ◇

43. Cynical, skeptical, and disillusioned with top management?　　　　　　　　YES ◇　　NO ◇

44. Hopeless, or convinced that they can't make a difference?　　　　　　　　　YES ◇　　NO ◇

45. Dissatisfied, hypercritical, and generally malcon-
tent?　　　　　　　　　　YES ◇　　NO ◇

Have you noticed:

46. That the company cares more about making a profit
than about the well-being of its employees?
　　　　　　　　　　　　　　YES ◇　　NO ◇

167

47. That the employees are useful only to the degree that they get their jobs done?   YES ◇   NO ◇

48. That favoritism takes priority over competence in career advancement?   YES ◇   NO ◇

49. Excessive absenteeism, low morale, high turnover, and unhappy employees?   YES ◇   NO ◇

50. That employees constantly work and strive but rarely experience completion and satisfaction?

YES ◇   NO ◇

QUIZ SCORING

In order to determine the degree to which your organization is affected by corporate negaholism, score two points for every "YES" answer.

Now total your score and find your corporation on the scale below. If your score is:

0   Congratulate yourself on being a part of a healthy, functioning organization where you can look forward to a productive and satisfying future.

1–24   Your organization has a mild case of corporate negaholism. While not perfect, the environment is functional and relatively healthy. It could be made even healthier through honest, direct communication, a commitment to confronting uncomfortable issues, and a willingness to honor the feelings of its employees.

25–40 Your organization has strong tendencies toward corporate negaholism. If you start now, you could clear up issues which might lead to an epidemic. Left unattended, they will grow into a chronic condition which will sooner or later affect the bottom line. A meeting of reliable and honorable employees to discuss the situation is the first step. The next step would be to diagnose the situation. Use the questionnaire to pinpoint the symptoms, then try to assess what the systemic causes are as differentiated from the symptoms. You might hire an organizational change agent to help you obtain an objective view.

41–60 You need to take your situation seriously. Without the proper measures, your organization is destined to become a certifiable negaholic corporation. Things have entered the danger zone, and active steps must be taken to rectify the situation. Things need to stabilize. Starting with a statement of purpose, a mission statement, and a list of goals and objectives, you need to get things back on track. You must address the process of decision-making, leadership, values, structure, training, strategy, interpersonal dynamics, priorities, and organizational culture. You must map out a master plan to address each issue and to ensure that all areas are covered in a methodical fashion.

61–80 The situation is critical. Priorities have been distorted, and the business is running you, not vice versa. The alarm has sounded, and it is time for the patient to have surgery and probably intensive care. You need a doctor! You have gone past the point of being able to "Do it yourself," and you need outside help. Don't worry about the cost, just get help. Get the best help you can find. You wouldn't worry about the expense if you needed open-heart surgery or to go to a detoxification center, so consider your business in the same way. You need to get back to basics, bring order out of chaos, and reorient yourself as to what you are really doing and why. It is possible to take back the reins and direct the business the way you want it to go, but emergency measures are required. Don't put this off, or you'll regret it.

81–100 Your organization is a negaholic corporation! Whether you are an employee, a director, or the chairman of the board, you need to come to terms with reality. You need to acknowledge this and take active measures to arrest a condition now beyond your control. The negativity is so subtle that you hardly even notice it; it has become the norm. You need a team of consultants, both internal and external (depending on the size of your organization), to bring you out of dysfunction and back into health. It is as if your organization is on its deathbed, and the only hope is CPR, a transfusion, and emergency surgery. There is hope if you take action now. Time is of the essence, since each day this condition is unattended to affects morale, attitude, production, teamwork, customer service, and especially the bottom line. Take action, keep your sense of humor, and move forward with the certainty that things can and will get better. Once you have acknowledged that there is a problem, there is hope for a solution.

◆　◆　◆

Depending upon your quiz score, you could be in one of several different situations. You might be ready to quit your job and leave corporate life forever. You may be actively recruiting an ally in the workplace to help you find a way through the land-mines and missiles. You could be worried about your situation, uncertain that your work environment will ever be nurturing or satisfying. Lastly, you could be excited that someone has written a book about your life at work, and hopeful that with a little outside help you can tackle your negaholic corporation and turn it around once and for all.

If you are a part of negaholic corporation, then you wrestle with negative attitudes, comments, and behaviors every day. You ask yourself, "Can I beat them or should I join them?" You battle with whether to become a corporate negaholic yourself or to take a stand and lead others toward a satisfying, meaningful, and productive future.

171

CHAPTER 7
◆
HOW DOES A COMPANY BECOME DYSFUNCTIONAL?

THE ORIGINS OF CORPORATE NEGAHOLISM

In the beginning there was a person who had a dream. The dream was to be self-employed. The dream was to have freedom from authority figures, the autonomy to make decisions, to make a lot of money, and to be able to enjoy all the wonderful things life has to offer. It was the American dream.

Translated into action, this dream often starts out auspiciously enough. For example, two young, aspiring entrepreneurs want to start their own business. They both have experience in the restaurant business. They have waited on tables, hosted, managed some of the more successful restaurants in the city, and feel that they can run their own restaurant just as well as those other guys, and maybe even better. They're tired of putting in endless hours, giving all they've got, and not reaping the rewards. Their days of working for someone else are over. They're ready to take the big risk; in fact, they feel that it's their turn to spin the wheel of fortune and success. After all this is America, and they want their chance to play big and win big. They are enthusiastic, confident almost to the point of arrogance, and want their turn at the big time.

Scott is a fashionplate who always looks like he stepped off the cover of *GQ* magazine. Dave, on the other hand, has a permanent five-o'clock shadow that gives him the look of someone who has been out prowling all night. Dave pays less attention to his clothes than to his aquariums and computers. Both men live in the fast lane, working hard and playing hard, with the assurance that there is nothing they can't do. They both really like each other, but more than that, they respect each other's abilities and differences and feel that they complement each other. They are very different in their styles, values, attitudes, and backgrounds, but they feel that this is all to their advantage. Scott is the people person who could charm the teeth off a barracuda, and Dave is the systems person who loves machines and gadgets. It looked like a winning combination on the surface.

Riding the crest of the wave, enlisting private investment and forming limited partnerships, they were putting together a multimillion-dollar enterprise right from the start. Enough people had seen them in action to believe that they really could do what they said. Business people, doctors, lawyers, and investors from all walks of life were handing over tens of thousands of dollars to get in on the ground floor.

Scott and Dave were smart and wanted to do things right. They hired the hottest architect in town, who produced a futuristic design for the first restaurant. The flagship site was on the trendiest street in town, and its location was in the center of all the activity. Since space was a real problem, they provided valet parking. The environment was high-tech, light, and up-tempo, the prototype from which hundreds of other restaurants would be copied. They searched for and found the perfect executive chef to compile a unique menu. The combination of Chinese/Thai food with no MSG, artificial additives, or cholesterol appealed alike to fans of health food, gourmets, oriental food lovers, and people on diets. The food was delicious and not terribly filling; you could consume great quantities without feeling full. It was also fun to eat, since people shared plates heaped high with tender morsels and participated with gusto in the feasting.

Scott and Dave had the uniforms designed so that they were bright, fun, and stylish. When they interviewed applicants, they made certain to take time to recruit the right ones. They wanted people who cared about other people, people who enjoyed making others happy by giving them what they wanted. They shared their vision with their waiters and hand-picked only the most friendly, enthusiastic, and positive ones.

They researched the market and found state-of-the-art hand-held computers which would input an order and transmit it to the kitchen simultaneously. They chose beverages which went well with the food, and had desserts designed to augment the overall concept. The seating arrangement was comfortable but didn't encourage lingering. With the handheld computers, waiters could deliver the average order within six minutes. With the seating design and the speed of the service, each table's turnaround averaged, forty-five minutes to an hour. The restaurant was open fourteen hours a day, seven days a week.

It seemed as if Scott and Dave had thought of everything. They had a clear vision: "To astonish guests throughout the world with our unmatched standards and passion for excellence in food, service, and environment." The concept had been fully developed, and they were planning to roll it out like McDonald's: the new "almost fast gourmet oriental health food" concept was going to take the world by storm. They were on their way, and everything was looking good.

The restaurant was an overnight success, they became rich and famous, and lived happily ever after. End of story, right? Well, not exactly. It's usually not all that simple. Even if you have the most positive and promising beginnings, things happen. Changes in the marketplace, economic fluctuations, changes in personnel, cash flow problems, discrepancies in management style, personality conflicts, and crises such as robberies, fires, union threats, and unexpected surprises complicate matters. The real test is not necessarily avoiding hurdles and snags, but rather how you deal with them when you encounter them. If you don't stop to examine your own personal dysfunctions and see how they could unconsciously affect you and your organization, then those same subtle dysfunctions can mark the demise of the organization. Scott and Dave never even considered that their personal dysfunctions would be a concern.

The first hurdle was raised by the employees, several of whom went to Scott complaining that they had a problem with Dave's management style. Dave was basically a Theory X type of guy. He liked to tell people what to do and then have them do it. He was straightforward and direct. Scott, on the other hand,

175

was primarily interested in having people operate harmoniously and happily on the job. He felt that if the employees were content, then their pleasant attitude would naturally be noted by the customers. Conversely, if the employees were not content, then their unhappy attitude would be served right along with the food. Scott liked to encourage self-management skills, autonomy, and initiative. He was more interested in the person than the task, while Dave was more interested in getting the job done. A basic difference in values: one valued relationships and the other valued task-management. In reality, both are essential for a business to succeed. This had never been an issue until three of the employees brought it to Scott's attention. Scott was dismayed, and felt that he and Dave should discuss the matter. It was a delicate issue, but it needed to be addressed now, before it grew into an even bigger concern.

Scott approached Dave over a lunch in which he carefully strategized his approach and timing. After they had completed their entrees, and before coffee, Scott broached the subject.

"Dave, there's something uncomfortable I need to talk to you about. It concerns our philosophy, personnel practices, and mostly our management styles. I want to discuss this in a sane, rational manner, and see if we can't resolve it easily and efficiently."

Dave appeared uneasy and nervous. His tone was defensive when he said that he was willing to address the topic at hand, and his demeanor communicated reticence. As Scott proceeded, Dave became more and more agitated. Finally he burst out: "Let's get to the point, Scott, who said what?"

Scott, who did not want to betray any confidences,

was leery. He responded, in a diplomatic and restrained manner, "It's not about indicting anyone, I just think it's time that we agreed how we are going to manage the staff. They're confused about who to go to, and they're trying to figure out which end is up. We just need to know what we want, and let them know it in a clear and effective manner."

Dave became increasingly defensive. "I know what I want, and I tell them all the time. I expect them to do what they're told, and right away. Now tell me, is there anything confusing about that?"

Scott felt disheartened and frustrated. He didn't know what to say to Dave. He internalized his feelings and berated himself for having clumsily mishandled the situation. He felt bad, and began to withdraw. The subject was closed for today. Perhaps on another day, with another strategy, things might go better.

After another several unsuccessful attempts, it was clear to Scott that they were at an impasse. He approached me to help the two of them resolve their differences. I agreed. I was eager to discover the origins of their management styles and to probe the rationale behind their actions. It was revelatory to learn from Dave and Scott about their personal histories. Dave was very candid in his response.

"My dad came out of the military, and he ran a tight ship. When he spoke we jumped. If you didn't do what you were told, you'd get your butt kicked. It was simple. Dad got results, and nobody dared question his authority. I guess I learned my management philosophy from watching and emulating him. After all, he was my idol; he could do no wrong."

Dave was right. He idolized his father and copied his style both consciously and unconsciously. He assumed that if it worked for his father it would work for him. His placed his dad on a pedestal, and he respected him more than anyone else, so it seemed only natural to emulate him in every way.

Scott was a different story. When I questioned him about his first experiences of being managed, he commented, "Both my parents worked, so we didn't see too much of them. My strongest relationship was with my mother. She was compassionate and would defend us against our father when he got angry. On the other hand, my mother wasn't particularly affectionate. She didn't shower us with hugs and kisses, and really wasn't emotionally available. My parents fought a lot, and to tell the truth, they drank a lot too. There were parties all the time at home, and people were often drunk. You know, when I look back on it I think my parents were really alcoholics. That's a tough accusation, but I can't remember a day when they didn't drink."

I pushed for management messages which he might have received from either parent. "My father was distant, inconsistent, and punitive," Scott answered. "There was no emotional connection with my dad. There were two sides to him: a distant one and an angry one. I preferred the distant side because the angry side terrified me. I did my best to stay out of his way. But, to answer your question, I decided that I didn't want to be anything like my father, and that I would follow in my mother's footsteps. I decided that I wanted to be compassionate, understanding, and fair. I wanted to be a good person and let people have a chance to grow and flourish under my guidance. In my family, the best I could do was survive. I guess I wanted to go beyond both of my parents and really make something of my life. I wanted to contribute to people's lives in a tangible way and have a positive impact on them."

Both Scott and Dave thought his respective management style was "normal," and for each of them it in fact was. Both of their management styles grew directly out of their respective early childhood experiences. Their philosophies, value judgments, and decisions reflected their early experiences. It was difficult for them to understand that their ways weren't the right way or the only way, but in fact were ways that they had learned through their parents' example. Since each of them thought he was right, both were convinced that the other person had to change. Working with them to sort out their differences was a challenging project.

I explained that there are many management styles, and that each has a place depending upon particular situations, people, and times. "If you have a fire, a crisis, or an emergency, then Dave's style is appropriate. When you have limited time and are under pressure to make an immediate decision without extensive data, Dave's style is extremely effective and appropriate." Dave felt justified, and gloated.

"On the other hand," I continued, "when you have sufficient time, are under moderate pressure, and have the opportunity to involve others in the decision-making process, then Scott's style—letting others take the initiative, own the decision, and implement the plan—is more effective in the long run. If you want permanent results, with your people owning their decisions, then you really have to go with a participative approach. You are both right, but you need to assess each situation individually, and do what is appropriate and will work in the long term for your business."

This was a relatively simple crisis for Dave and Scott,

since it involved basic principles of situational leadership. Resolution ensued with the willingness of both parties. The dysfunction which surfaced between Scott and Dave revolved around their inability to address and successfully deal with issues critical to the effective functioning of their corporation. That they perceived a crisis and were willing to call in an outsider to help resolve it demonstrated their commitment to addressing their lack of alignment and their desire to find a solution. The outcome was satisfactory. They were both willing to learn from each other, to give and take, and to relinquish their initial positions to find a mutually agreeable solution.

As the relationship between Scott and Dave developed, other matters surfaced. Dave did not change his style overnight, nor did Scott. It was a process which called for a great deal of communication and a willingness to resolve issues.

Dave walked into the office one day and announced that he and Suzy, the woman he lived with, were going to Bali for ten days. Scott began to seethe inside. Scott didn't say anything, but instead internalized his feelings as he had before. He got up, walked out, and slammed the door. Dave thought, "What's gotten into him?"

Scott thought to himself, "He never considers me when he makes decisions. What if I wanted to take my vacation at the same time, then what would he say? Besides, this is the third vacation he's taken this year, and I haven't taken one. He says it's research for the business, but really, how much restaurant research can you do in Bali? He did this same thing the other day when he told the employees that they had to be here twenty minutes before their shifts. He didn't discuss it with me, he didn't even inform me about it, and then when Mary came to me to ask me why we had this new rule, I didn't have a clue as to what she was talking about. I looked like an idiot, uninformed about my own company. He goes off half-cocked and decides whatever he wants about policies, procedures, and systems, and it doesn't even occur to him to consider me. He did the same thing with the computer system. One day he decided that we needed a computer system, so he went out and spent ten thousand dollars on one. I found out after it was all over. Sometimes I don't feel like a partner at all, but more like an employee who works for Dave."

The reason Scott was seething with rage had less to do with the immediate situation than with the accumulation of many similar incidents which had been swept under the carpet. The build-up of unexpressed emotions had culminated in this explosion. He hadn't addressed his feelings about the computer situation, or the twenty-minute check-in policy, or several other acts Dave had performed autonomously. The trip to Bali triggered a reaction disproportionate to the stimulus. Suddenly, all the pent-up, unexpressed emotions welled up in him, and he could hardly contain his feelings. The slammed door was his first outward expression of displeasure.

When Dave asked Scott what was bothering him, Scott said, "Nothing, I just didn't know you were planning on going to Bali."

"I didn't either," said Scott, "We just decided. You're the first to know."

"What if I'm planning on leaving town at the same time?" Scott retorted.

"Then we'll figure something out. Why are you getting all bent out of shape about this Bali thing? What's the big deal anyway?" Dave reasoned.

"It's not just Bali, it's everything. You never ask me

what I think. You never talk to me before you make decisions. Look at the twenty-minute rule you implemented without even considering me. Here I am, the director of operations, and I don't know what's going on." Scott's tone grew more intense.

"What are you talking about? We talked about the staff being late for shifts, you knew we were dealing with that problem. I just figured out a way to get it solved—it happened in a conversation with the assistant managers, quite casually. What's the big deal again?"

"It's the same thing with the computers. I turn around one day and you've spent ten thousand dollars on a computer system which you never discussed with me. Tell me the truth, am I your partner or am I your lackey?" Scott said indignantly.

"Hey, what are you getting all worked up about? Look, we needed a computer system, you're not into computers, and I had to get the job done. I heard about a good deal, and I had to act fast. It was as simple as that. I got the best system for our needs at the best price. Either you trust me or you don't. Which is it?" Dave said.

Scott took three deep breaths. "It's not a question of trust, it's about being fully informed and active in the decision-making process. If we're partners, I should be a part of the decision-making process, especially when it involves spending big bucks."

Dave was task-oriented, impatient, and committed to getting results. Scott wanted to make decisions jointly, especially when they entailed large capital expenditures. They had not resolved their decision-making process and were in conflict because their different orientations did not mesh. They had never addressed it before, and now it had become an issue. To have differences is normal; the challenge is learning to resolve them in a healthy way. Dave's tendency to operate autonomously was excluding his partner not only from the decision-making process but also from the dialogue which assesses priorities, timing, and the allocation of funds. If the two had discussed areas of responsibility and parameters of authority, and delegated the computer area to Dave, then things would have been different. As it was, they had to sit down and close the rift between them.

The small, one-of-a-kind restaurant grew, and Scott and Dave expanded their operation into five different franchises within eighteen months. During rapid growth they operated more often than not from a crisis-management orientation. Neither one did a lot of planning, anticipating, or organizing, nor did they stop and take time out to resolve their differences. They kept ploughing ahead, putting out fires, and having occasional flare-ups which the employees would watch in fascination. When they reached an impasse, they would call me in as a neutral person to help them resolve their differences.

The partners had agreed that Dave would be responsible for recruiting more capital to open new stores and that Scott would be in charge of operations. One day, Scott came into one of the franchises and found Dave giving orders to several of the waiters and busboys. In fact, the orders he was giving were contrary to the ones Scott had given two days earlier. Dave was overstepping his boundaries. Scott was dismayed and at a loss for what to say.

When he had collected his thoughts, Scott approached Dave and asked, "Didn't we agree that I was to have all the responsibility for operations?"

Dave replied nonchalantly, "Of course we did, but

you wouldn't want me to come in here and ignore what's going on, would you? That would be irresponsible of me. Besides, what kind of partner would be so narrow-minded as to focus only on his own work and not on what needed attention at the moment?"

Scott was becoming more irate by the minute. "But you gave them directives that went against everything I said. You didn't check with me first, you just barged in like a bull in a china shop, without any regard for my instructions."

"Hey, I did what I thought was right. It seemed like the right thing at the moment. If you want me to apologize, I will. I'm sorry, O.K.? Now can we get on with it?"

Scott called me and confessed how difficult it was for him to confront Dave. He said that he usually felt squashed or deflated when he tried to get something resolved. He was rarely satisfied by his attempts to resolve conflicts.

HOW CONTAGION SPREADS THROUGHOUT AN ORGANIZATION

After four years, Dave and Scott had a crisis on their hands. The employees were severely disillusioned and mistrusted management, and morale problems were rampant. There were credibility and communication gaps between management and waiters, a cold war between waiters and busboys, and indifference between the waiters and the customers. Even though the waiters knew that their tips were in direct proportion to how well they served the public, their resentment and hostility towards the owners and managers was spilling over to their interactions with the customers. When Bradley, a waiter, asked Dave why they no longer accepted American Express cards, he was told, "We just don't. It's a new policy." So when the next customer asked Bradley the same question, he curtly replied, "That's our policy!" He was passing on to the customer what he had received from Dave: "That's just the way it is, got it? Now don't ask me again!" The overflow of negativity was affecting the bottom line. The wider the communication gaps grew between Scott and Dave, the more they were passed on to the individual store managers and subsequently on to the employees, and the more unpleasant the interactions became between service personnel and customers. Business was dropping off radically. At this point Dave called me to see if I had any bright ideas.

First I met with Scott and Dave to help them with many issues that had been left unresolved by their unwillingness to compromise, their general inability, and their crisis-management style. Neither Scott nor Dave wanted to hear what the employees had to say. Scott was fearful of being attacked; Dave was basically uninterested in the employees' attitudes and feelings. Addressing these concerns with the two of them, I said quite frankly, "If you are uninterested or too fearful, then it just won't work. You really need to care about your employees' feelings, concerns, and ideas to the same degree that you want them to care about your customers' needs."

They wanted to go ahead, and so we proceeded. We began by meeting with the staff. We met with the most difficult staff members individually, and all the rest in small groups. Their individual feelings and reactions included fear, mistrust, covert hostility, resentment, and deep-seated hurt. It was necessary to coax out their withheld thoughts and feelings in order to see what could be rectified.

The employees mistrusted management because when they tried to communicate they never saw any results. Their concerns seemed to bounce off deaf ears. They were tired of the inconsistencies, the radical mood-swings, the changes in direction, and the reactive crisis-management. "One day we spend thousands of dollars on tropical fish and expensive fishtanks for the rest-rooms in the restaurants or one of the partners goes out and buys a jet ski, and the next day money is too tight to buy tops for the teapots," one said in frustrated tones. Several had asked about insurance benefits but they were told that "it's not in the budget." But when they saw truckloads of merchandise arriving (anything with the company logo on it, from ashtrays to T-shirts, sold briskly at each franchise), they felt unimportant and resentful.

There were cutbacks and layoffs juxtaposed with lavish parties; one day it was champagne for everyone, and the next day the employee meal was cut in half. The employees were confused and upset. This was not the company they came to work for. Things had changed, and not for the better.

We decided to institute a program entitled "Excellence in Customer Service." In this program, the employees had the opportunity to openly and freely communicate their concerns, frustrations, desires, and expectations. I insisted that a management representative be present at every session to hear what was being said, and to make a commitment to take action, execute the task, and agree to a time-line in order to produce the desired result: the restoration of management's credibility. Scott, Dave, and the general manager made a commitment to report to me every thirty days with what had been accomplished, what the tangible results were, and what the status was of all the other projects.

The sessions worked well. Management listened to what was being said and responded to it in a nondefensive manner. The follow-through was thorough; the employees saw results and began to trust in management's commitment to them.

Scott and Dave still had their bad moments. Dave reminded Scott of his father, and Scott reminded Dave of his mother. When Dave became distant and angry, Scott became a small boy cowering in front of his father. When Scott talked about caring for the employees, Dave would hear his mother and tune out whatever he was saying.

The business did succeed, although there were some rocky parts along the road. Scott and Dave nearly split apart many times, and each would have walked away thinking he was right. Since they had made a commitment to work through the issues, however, they were willing to go beyond the easy way out—blaming the other person, finger-pointing, and fault-finding—to discover what their dysfunctional behaviors were, and to learn the lessons which would help them become healthy and functional in all parts of their lives.

LESSONS FOR MANAGEMENT

Scott, Dave, and the other managers learned from some of the mistakes they had made. They learned never to promise something if you can't deliver. They learned to listen more effectively, to document what someone says, and to encourage him to get everything off his chest. Listening alone is not enough, although it is a critical step toward the final resolution. An employee needs to personally experience that he has been heard, that what he has to say matters to someone. He needs to feel that his presence makes a difference.

Management learned that three things are necessary in dealing with disgruntled employees: listening until all the issues are aired, feeding back what was heard and understood from listening, and then jointly finding solutions to each one of the concerns. All too often, we mis-hear or misunderstand what someone is trying to communicate. We listen through a filter, a smoke screen constructed out of our own experiences, feelings, or judgments, and then categorize what the person is saying. Feedback is critical. It is also extremely validating to hear your words repeated by a listener. In order for a person to feel really heard, we, as listeners, need to suspend judgment, drop all defensive attitudes, and hear what he is saying, feeling, and also what he is *not* saying. Very often, body language will communicate more than the words.

After the listening and feedback phases, next comes the follow-through. People need to see results. You can actively listen to someone until the end of time, but your credibility will be destroyed if you don't follow through with tangible results. If the employees say they need more spoons to get their jobs done, then the lack of spoons needs to be addressed. If spoons are needed, spoons must be provided. If spoons are not provided, then a legitimate and satisfactory reason should be given for their absence. Promises should only be made when they can be honored. Management needs to make its word as valuable as gold.

When employees can track the process from communication to discussion to plan of action to result, they begin to believe in management. Management then demonstrates that it is trustworthy and credible. Employees feel as if they matter. They notice that someone is attentive to their concerns. They feel important and deserving of having their needs and wants met.

In four months, the management team and I witnessed a veritable transformation in Scott and Dave's business. Employees who had been disillusioned, skeptical, cynical, and overtly hostile had changed radically. They were now open, trusting, willing, eager, participative, and even enthusiastic. If you looked at the same group at the beginning of the project and then again at the end, you wouldn't have believed your eyes.

These profound changes were the result of:

◆ Management caring enough to do something about the situation.
◆ Management's commitment to seeing the project through to the end.
◆ The willingness of everyone to actively listen.
◆ The desire to suspend judgment.
◆ Taking the situation seriously.
◆ Focusing on solutions, not dwelling on problems.
◆ The willingness of the employees to communicate.
◆ The willingness of the employees to work with management in finding solutions.
◆ Pressing to get to the crux of the situation.
◆ Follow-through on task-management.
◆ Everyone involved being accountable for the outcome.
◆ Management making only promises that could be delivered.
◆ Management caring enough to invest time, energy, and money.

CHAPTER 8

◆

THE TEN CHARACTERISTICS OF DYSFUNCTIONAL COMPANIES

All negaholic companies have certain key characteristics in common. The function of a work environment is to provide the proper conditions for the manufacture, marketing, and sale of products or services to the customer. Certain organizations are designed to make a profit while others are not. Any attitudes, behaviors, or activities which impede, restrict, or prohibit the group from fulfilling its purpose are dysfunctional elements. The dysfunctions may be localized in a department, in individuals, or in the cellular structure of the organization as a whole.

When an organization has the dysfunction of being extremely demanding, perfectionistic, and unreasonable, it is difficult for unsuspecting people to discern if they are being treated fairly or being used and manipulated for the desired outcomes of the organization rather than for their own growth and well-being. The desire to be liked, to be part of the team, and to be fulfilled is so important to individuals who come from dysfunctional homes that their ability to discriminate and perceive situations clearly is impaired.

Dysfunctional work environments attract people from dysfunctional homes. They are attracted to the familiarity and essential association with home and family. If it looks like home and feels like home, it probably *is* home. Home is defined as an environment which is dear to one because of the feelings of familiarity, comfort, and security it provides. Whether the family of origin was healthy or dysfunctional, it created the fundamental imprinting which the child/adult relates to as his essential frame of reference. The frame of reference is that set of associations, thoughts, feelings, beliefs, attitudes, decisions, and behaviors which forms the pivotal point of relation to the outside world. The frame of reference is so much a part of a person's reality that it seems like a part of his skin. It may not be positive, desirable, or preferable, but it is an integral personality component.

Employees frequently find themselves working for bosses who remind them of one of their parents. If the parents were supportive and empowering, employees flourish under the boss's guidance, and the relationship works out well. But if the parents were neglectful, diminishing, perfectionistic, abusive, inconsistent, unavailable, compulsive, unconfronting, addictive, controlling, indirect, overly protective, or unconfrontable, then the child/adult/employee will be unconsciously drawn to these types of behavior. If left unconscious, childhood patterns of behavior will simply repeat themselves over and over again. Even if the employee leaves the undesirable work situation and goes to another job, he will probably be drawn to the same kind of person and/or situation that he has just left.

If the situation is dealt with sensitively, then the old patterns of childhood behavior can be changed and new behaviors chosen which represent the adult's preferences. All situations can be changed, and all old wounds can eventually be healed. In order to effectively change yourself or your situation, you need to have the belief in, the commitment to, and the desire and willingness to achieve the end result. In order to change dysfunctional behaviors, you need to look at them, see them in the proper perspective, determine a healthy way of dealing with each one, set out on the path to functioning and health, and be supported on the way.

There are ten characteristics which are consistently true of dysfunctional companies. All dysfunctional companies have at least one, and usually three or more of the following:

1. A tendency to avoid or deny the reality of an unpleasant situation.
2. An excessive need for control over situations, environments, and individuals.
3. A tendency toward secrecy, indirect communication, and collusion.
4. Avoidance, denial, suppression, and discounting of all emotions which are inappropriate to the work environment, such as love, hate, anger, sadness, and excitement. This is determined by the individual culture.
5. An inability to address and successfully deal with issues critical to the effective functioning of the corporation.

6. A protective attitude geared toward guarding taboo topics and ensuring their secrecy.
7. An overriding loyalty to the corporation which manifests itself in a desire to preserve, protect, and perpetuate the status quo of the organization, and to avoid any radical changes even if they are for the ultimate health of the organization.
8. An inability to be consistent in moods, behavior, attitudes, policies, and decision-making style.
9. Rigidity in thinking. A binary approach to problem-solving.
10. Compulsive behavior: overly perfectionist, conscientious, and orderly.

A TENDENCY TO AVOID OR DENY THE REALITY OF AN UNPLEASANT SITUATION

The inability to confront unpleasant issues is at the top of the list of dysfunctional behaviors. In dysfunctional environments, avoidance and denial are very commonplace. In order to achieve resolution on any particular issue, you have to be willing to examine that issue, come to terms with it, see what lessons are to be learned from the situation, and determine what steps you are willing to take to resolve it.

Stephanie, the CEO of one franchise in a chain of furniture stores, knew that something was wrong. She had a feeling in her stomach that told her she needed to pay closer attention to the company finances, but she brushed it off by saying that the accounting staff was thoroughly competent and that there was no need to worry. Four months later, she discovered that, unbeknownst to her, bonuses had been given to key personnel. In addition, expensive gifts had been bestowed on others without her knowledge or authorization. She was livid with rage. She stormed into the chief financial officer's office and demanded an explanation. When the CFO was interrogated, she said that everything had been submitted in the budget. Stephanie was dismayed, disheartened, and felt betrayed.

Stephanie had to figure out a plan which would attend to both the immediate situation and the long-range solution. The immediate situation which she was concerned about related to policies, parameters of authority, and unauthorized expenditures. She wanted to address the need for clear policies which could not be misinterpreted, and she also wanted to take a closer look at what she could learn from the situation. How did her own personal dysfunctions relate to her professional responsibilities? What was the learning opportunity here for Stephanie?

Stephanie realized that an important truth had never been recognized. She had denied the reality of her own situation. She saw that she needed to confront head-on the issue she had been avoiding. The truth was that she had never felt able in the financial area, had deferred all accounting and bookkeeping matters to others whom she felt were more competent and hoped that everything would turn out all right. By avoiding the situation she had created an even bigger problem. A part of her wanted to simply replace her CFO and delegate the problem to someone else. A larger part of her, however, knew that merely replacing the person would only perpetuate the pattern. She was ready to deal with her role in the master puzzle.

By examining all angles, she could tackle both the form and the substance of the problem. To become fully functional, she needed to issue a new and clear policy on wage-administration and gift-giving, implement systems including checks and balances, and recruit her CPA to give her personal tutoring in financial management. This way she could handle the immediate situation, confront her dysfunctional area, overcome her Achilles heel, deal directly with her weakness, and become proficient in an area where previously she had felt weak.

It was fascinating to learn about Stephanie's family of origin and the roots of her dysfunction. Stephanie had been raised in a well-off family whose members were pleasant, charming, and only discussed happy topics. Everyone was kind and loving with each other, even to the point of concealing what was really going on. When Stephanie was entering puberty, her mother ran away with a younger man. It came as quite a shock to the entire family. No one had suspected that there was a problem with the marriage. Stephanie's mother, a gourmet cook, excelled in everything she tried her hand at. From tennis to planning events, from needlework to the Christmas trimmings, she was the model mother and the spirit of enthusiasm.

Stephanie's family did not address unpleasant subjects. She had acquired that trait and acted it out in the financial area of her business. Dysfunctional behavior doesn't necessarily occur under the same conditions under which it was acquired, but rather exhibits itself haphazardly. Stephanie's dysfunction remained unrecognized until she took a close look at her life. When she chose to examine her past and present, she brought the unconscious patterns of behavior to the forefront, and was able to take a new direction and be released from her old behaviors.

A HIGH NEED FOR CONTROL OVER SITUATIONS, ENVIRONMENTS, AND INDIVIDUALS

Since individuals in dysfunctional homes have little or no control over their childhood environment, it stands to reason that as adults they would want to exert a lot of control in their present circumstances in order to feel secure and create a sense of predictability. In work environments, this can be problematic if the objective is to work as a team.

Two writers who collaborate in leading seminars together had a partnership teaching publishing. The team taught seminars for sixteen to twenty people at a time. Every time Dean would speak about Mimi's side of the business, she would grimace and correct him. He was constantly saying inaccurate things and she was always ready to correct him. He would say, "Mimi has been in the business five or six years," and she would mumble, under breath, "Seven!" He would say that she had written eight books, and she would pop back, "Ten."

She felt embarrassed, and he felt irritated. He simply couldn't get the facts straight, and it drove her crazy. The more she corrected him, the more inaccurate and clumsy he became with the facts. This dynamic went on continuously. It wasn't a major problem, since they only taught together six times a year, but it continued to bother them both.

In order for Mimi and Dean to overcome their non-supportive dynamic, they had to take it seriously enough to discuss it openly. They had to want to clear up the issue and resolve it once and for all. Once they were willing to address it, they made some interesting discoveries.

Upon closer examination, it became clear that Mimi had been raised in a home with an overbearing mother and a shy and retiring father. Her mother dictated what everyone should do and how it should be done. Her mother was clearly in control and tried to run Mimi's life. Her father was merely a shadow who faded into the background. As an adult, Mimi felt a great need for control over situations and people. The embarrassment she had felt over her mother's behavior made her hypersensitive to other embarrassing situations. She was always concerned about how people perceived her, especially in terms of her close associations with others. When Dean made mistakes, she wanted to set the record straight so that people would not hear inconsistencies and think that they didn't know what they were doing. She was afraid that people would discover that they couldn't agree on the basic facts. If they weren't aligned on how long they had been in business, then they were really screwed up!

Dean, conversely, had little concern for details and found them irrelevant and unnecessary. He made little effort to remember facts and figures accurately because they were never a high priority with him. In childhood, one of the ways he got attention was by giving wrong answers or saying things inaccurately. When he gave the right answer, he heard a simple, "That's correct." This pattern extended into adulthood, and was now being reenacted with his partner.

When Dean and Mimi dismantled their pattern of mistake-and-correct, they discovered that they didn't want to be doing either one. Mimi didn't want to spend her time correcting Dean, and Dean didn't want to be making gaffes which Mimi would feel a need to correct. The answer was in both of them seeing what lay behind their behavior. Mimi vowed to stop correcting Dean, even if he were wrong. She resolved each time to write down the error and put a note about it in his basket, and he could choose to read it or not. Dean was going to make a concerted effort to only use numbers which he knew were correct; if he were unsure, he would turn to Mimi first and ask her the question: "How many years have you been in business now?" This way it became not his problem or her problem, but *their* problem. Since it was their problem, they both had to rectify the situation together.

A TENDENCY TOWARD SECRECY, INDIRECT COMMUNICATION, AND COLLUSION

Ted was the director of marketing, Tyler the director of sales, and Derek the only vice president of a huge soap-product conglomerate. Derek had a conversation with Ted in which he told him that Tyler's consumer-products division was being phased out of the business. Ted was surprised and deliberately altered his strategy to incorporate these facts. He was preoccupied with this information and couldn't stop thinking about its ramifications. He didn't dare tell Tyler about his communication with Derek because it was confidential. Ted's behavior toward Tyler changed in that he began acting more guarded and withdrawn. He thought more and said less. Whenever plans for the expansion or development of Tyler's area were under discussion, Ted would clam up and withdraw. He was constantly figuring out how he could design marketing plans which would exclude Tyler's area and at the same time not let the cat out of the bag. He became very anxious, and carried on an interior monologue that sounded something like this:

"If I exclude the consumer-products division from the marketing plan, Tyler will know something is up."

"Yeah, but if I include it, it will add hundreds of virtually useless hours to my workload."

"Yeah, but I'm not supposed to know the information I'm privy to."

"But I can't forget what I already know. It's useless extra work."

"Just get your job done, and stop all the double thinking."

"Sure, but how can I do my job knowing what I know?"

"Just pretend that you don't know anything."

"Easier said than done. I don't know what to do!"

It was inappropriate for Derek to have divulged to Ted information which made him ineffective on the job. After a closer look at Derek's motivation, some things became clear. Derek came from a family of six children. Both parents engaged in triangular communication. The parents would never go directly to any child and address his or her behavior directly; instead, George would go to Hal and discuss Lily, and Lily in turn would have a conversation with Jean about George. Hal would talk to Blake about Jean, and so on. In other words, Derek's orientation was to talk about people, not to them. He had no experience of talking to people about issues which pertained to them, and in fact it was an alien concept to him. Contacting Ted to discuss Tyler was his standard way of operating, and he had no idea that this was dysfunctional behavior.

As it turned out, no one was willing to tackle this dysfunction. Ted was transferred to corporate Siberia, and the dysfunction was relegated to another territory. Derek kept his dysfunctional behaviors, and Ted kept his consumer-products division. If the dysfunctional behavior of a person is too uncomfortable to address, then people usually find ways to either work around him or eject him altogether from their immediate sphere of influence.

AVOIDANCE, DENIAL, SUPPRESSION, AND DISCOUNTING OF ALL EMOTIONS INAPPROPRIATE TO THE BUSINESS ENVIRONMENT

Delbert, the claims manager of a large insurance company, was trying his best to run his department. His wife was pregnant and on doctor's orders was confined to bed. Del was worried about his wife, her health, and the health of their first baby. Eventually, Clara went into labor and gave birth. Tragically, the baby was born with a respiratory disease and had to have respiratory support in order to live. Both parents were exhausted by the hard pregnancy, the difficult delivery, and now the painful reality of having a child who needed constant medical attention.

Del felt alone. He felt he needed to care for his wife, who was traumatized by the event and held herself personally responsible for the condition of the child. He felt he didn't have time to attend to his own pain, loss, and sadness. He was suffering from the financial burdens of high medical bills and his wife's inability to be a wage-earner after the birth. His evenings and weekends were spent taking care of his wife and baby and dealing with all the domestic issues which didn't get handled all week. He felt as if he were four different people: his wife's caretaker, the new father of a baby in need of constant medical attention, the domestic support person, and the manager of the claims department. With all of these roles and responsibilities, there was little time for Del to take care of Del.

At work Del had little or no opportunity to feel, experience, and express the feelings which were wreaking havoc on him. After all, he was supposed to leave his personal problems at home, come to work, and do his job. In order to be professional he had to get the job done, and set aside his personal life, his feelings, concerns, worries, and anxieties about his family. His boss was sympathetic, but at the same time he had to turn out a quality work product and couldn't afford to be "soft."

There were times on the job when Del would space out and lose his train of thought. After a minute or so he would suddenly come to and tune back in to the present situation. Other times he would snap at people, who then responded with alarm because his extreme reaction seemed inappropriate to the stimulus. He was irritable and emotionally inconsistent. He was having trouble concentrating, his own health wasn't good, and he was steadily gaining weight.

When I probed to see where Del's values had originated, I found out that his father, an undertaker, had set very high standards for the whole family. The family was strict, and you were supposed to be a totally selfless person who only thought about others, not about yourself. Emotions were not valued. The belief was that whatever trials you were given were blessings which showed how special you were. The greater the suffering and trial, the more you were loved.

Del fit well into his work environment because the

firm did not condone feelings being expressed on the job, and neither did Del's belief-system. Del was suffering but, because of the culture and his own beliefs, he was both unwilling and unable to get in touch with his feelings. Now and then he would simply break down, but these moments were usually at home after everyone else was in bed asleep. When his emotions took over and he became overwhelmed, he couldn't understand what was going on with him. At times he wondered whether he were going crazy, but those moments too passed.

AN INABILITY TO ADDRESS AND SUCCESSFULLY DEAL WITH ISSUES CRITICAL TO THE EFFECTIVE FUNCTIONING OF THE CORPORATION

Three women were partners in a successful accessories company. Casey, Beth, and Lynette were the best of friends and had a great time doing business together. Casey had started the firm, and then later Beth and Lynette bought into it. In addition to having fun, they also made money. They had a staff of twenty-five and gross sales of several million. They were well on their way to joining the Fortune 500.

Casey was in charge of designs, Lynette was responsible for marketing the product, and Beth was the chief financial officer. Every year they doubled their gross, and the company was growing like mad. It expanded too rapidly, however, and Beth couldn't keep up with the work. She started falling behind in her financial reports, and because Casey was overwhelmed and Lynette was on the road, they let it slide. At first the financials were a few days late, then two weeks late, then a month late, then they stopped coming altogether.

Casey and Lynette wanted to say something to Beth, so they decided to have a meeting. When they confronted Beth with the absence of the financials, she became defensive and gave all kinds of reasons and excuses to justify her actions. The first meeting was less than satisfying. Beth made promises, and eventually the financials showed up. But by the time they arrived they were out of date and useless.

In the second meeting, Casey and Lynette again confronted Beth with the tardiness of the financials, and again Beth was less than receptive. Casey and Lynette were dismayed and awaited the results. No behavior change. Finally, they decided that a third try was worth the risk.

In the third meeting, Casey and Lynette asked how they could support Beth in getting her job done. In the discussion that ensued, it became clear that Beth was a self-sufficient type who did everything on her own and had a great deal of pride as well as difficulty in reaching out for support. After all, Beth had been a financial consultant to other organizations and should be able to run her own. Beth said that she pressured herself to do her job, do it right, and never ask for help. She was self-sufficient and would break all of her teeth biting the bullet before she would cry "Uncle." Things started to make more sense to Casey and Lynette, and at this point they decided they had better look at their own behavior and see what childhood patterns they themselves were locked into.

When they hired my consulting firm, we discovered some interesting childhood patterns. Both Casey and Lynette came from families with three daughters each. As children they had both paired up with their closest sibling in collusion against the third. Casey and Lynette were shocked to see how they had re-created their childhood situation, with Beth being their third sibling in the business. Casey and Lynette's pattern played directly into Beth's pattern of self-sufficiency, which in turn caused the organization to suffer. In order to unblock the stalemate and align their efforts with functional behavior, they had to break the old patterns.

Beth was the only girl in a family of three children, and was extremely good at math. She was revered by all the members of her family and was looked to as the bright child who was wise beyond her years. She was put on a pedestal and isolated by her two brothers, who always played sports together and excluded her. She was always in search of situations where she could operate autonomously, be respected for her expertise, and lauded for her financial creativity. She had been the comptroller of a major city, but still her pattern of autonomy and solitude prevailed. She was just not a team player.

Beth had to stop being so self-sufficient, tell the truth about her situation, and reach out for support. She had to be willing to say, "I'm over my head. I need help. I can't get my job done." Then, when support was offered, she had to be willing to accept it. On the other hand, Casey had to be willing to roll up her sleeves and actually crunch the numbers with her. Casey had to learn what she previously had relegated to Beth's area.

Lynette then asked Beth to coach her in the financial area. Lynette admitted that in order to feel O.K. in her family, she had to align herself with her little sister. She had had very little in common with and felt alienated from her oldest sister, who had majored in economics. Her older sister, Betty, was so distant from her that she decided mathematical people were in general peculiar and too different from her to be close to. All in all, she felt inadequate around them and judged them negatively so that she didn't have to look at her own insecurities.

Lynette was grateful for the illumination, as were Casey and Beth. Since they had unearthed what was really going on, they were released from the chains of the past that had locked them into automatic behavior patterns. After having discovered their unconscious decisions, they were free to choose how they wanted to handle these situations in the future. The business became stronger as a result of their efforts to understand each other and themselves.

A PROTECTIVE ATTITUDE GEARED AT GUARDING TABOO TOPICS AND ENSURING THEIR SECRECY

A buyer for an old, established department store chain was married to the vice president of marketing in corporate headquarters. He had a fight with the president, and subsequently was abruptly terminated. A wave of concern spread throughout the organization, with mutterings in the cubicles as to why it happened and if it were justified. Bea, the vice president's wife, continued to work for the company, almost as if nothing had happened. Her cheerful attitude and professional demeanor camouflaged her carefully guarded secret feelings. Within eighteen months, her husband, Garrett, filed suit against the company for unfair termination. People were shocked that he would sue the mother company. The reverberations spread throughout the organization. Nothing like this had ever happened before. Management was appalled that Bea would continue working for the company while her husband was suing it. Employees were torn between their loyalty toward her, her husband, and the company. People felt they had to take sides, and yet they didn't want to. Many employees, including Bea, felt like little children torn between two parents going through a difficult divorce: unable to do anything, and feeling the strained undercurrent.

The dysfunction of not being able to discuss issues critical to the company was at the core of this uncomfortable situation. The corporate attorneys added to the tension by mandating that no one discuss the case on the job. The reason for this edict was to ensure that Bea didn't gather more evidence of her husband's competency. As a result of the mystery surrounding this issue, no one could think of anything else. People would talk in hushed tones in quiet corridors and behind closed doors. In a sense it was like a dark family secret, well known but never openly acknowledged.

Bea came from a family full of pioneer spirit. You kept your head high, held the tears in, and never showed your weaknesses. She was used to being a stoic and holding the family together. No matter how tough circumstances were, she never let anyone know the toll they took on her. She had seen her family through tough times and had never complained. Her father had been accused of embezzlement and was investigated. She had to go to school and face the disdainful looks and comments of her peers, which intimidated her but trained her well for the years which followed. Although her father's record was ultimately cleared, she never forgot how the incident made her feel.

Bea felt loyal to her husband as well as to the company. She was torn between love of her family and love of her job. Her husband's abrupt dismissal forced her to relive her childhood experience of humiliation and shame. She had learned how to cope in her early years. She knew how to stand tall, hold her head high, and maintain her dignity. She knew how to maintain the front, but deep inside she ached. She felt the pain in quiet solitary moments late at night.

Bea ultimately left the company, and with her devoted husband moved to her dream city, Paris. She got a job working for a designer as the coordinator of her different collections all over the world. She was blissfully happy, and delighted to have left the really painful parts of her life behind. Throughout all the stress, she maintained her dignity and transcended her difficult past.

In the end, taboo subjects feed a dysfunctional system. Forbidden topics may range from a discrepancy in pay scale to selling drugs to secret affairs to embezzling funds. The number of topics is limitless and engulfs the past, the present, and the future. You can tell a topic is taboo because of the uneasy feeling that you get when bringing it up, or the way people pounce upon a juicy piece of gossip about it. If you receive looks that could kill when you mention it, or if someone else brings up something and you cringe inside, then you are on to a hot one. The minute people sense a forbidden subject, they become obsessed with it. First of all they want to be in on the scoop. Second, they want to find out all the details. Then rumors start to fly, and with each telling become more preposterous. People always assume the worst, and their telling and retellings are evidence of their wild imaginings. Secrets tend to segregate those who know from those who don't. If you know you're "in," and if you don't you're on the outside wishing you knew. All in all, people become consumed with chatter that has nothing to do with work.

AN OVERRIDING LOYALTY TO THE CORPORATION THAT MANIFESTS ITSELF IN A DESIRE TO PRESERVE, PROTECT, AND PERPETUATE THE STATUS QUO OF THE ORGANIZATION, AND TO AVOID ANY RADICAL CHANGES EVEN IF THEY ARE FOR THE ULTIMATE HEALTH OF THE ORGANIZATION

A large and diversified multinational holding company was going through a major organizational change. The top brass at corporate headquarters were deciding what to do about the drop in revenues. They determined that their only hope was to cut back on costs and initiate major layoffs. They asked the CEO and the key VP's to make a tour of the company's different divisions and deliver the news in a speech rather than in a corporate memo. This personal touch, they thought, would show care and a commitment to their employees as individuals. Since the news would come straight from the horse's mouth, no false rumors could start.

A trip to fifteen cities was planned, the speech was written, and the schedules were cleared. After the third speech, there was a tremor throughout the organization. Walter, the CEO, was dismayed that his plan wasn't working. Employees were cynical and sarcastic about the whole reorganization and the "trim the fat campaign," as it was called. He tried to investigate the cause of the unrest and resistance to the new plan, but people were reluctant to share the truth with him.

Finally, Walter got one of his inside people to divulge the truth. While Walter was giving his "trim the fat" speech, the limousines which had ushered the executives there were parked nearby with the engines running and the limo drivers standing by. This tended to cast a shadow on the credibility of the entire project. After the buzzing started, more rumors quickly began to circulate: in the midst of the lean times, all of the executives were still flying first class, and the cutbacks were really only happening in the field, not at corporate headquarters; the whole cutback scheme was brought about by a series of bad acquisitions which could now not be easily sold off; the company had overextended its international investments, and quite frankly had bitten off more than it could chew; the employees, who had nothing to do with the unwise acquisitions, were now being sacrificed to atone for the sins of top management.

The dysfunctional loyalty that management felt toward the status quo and its desire to preserve its own jobs led it to support an unwise decision to cut back expenses and lay off employees. As a result of management's avoidance of its real problems, the truth wasn't told, innocent people were sacrificed, and the plan ultimately backfired. Management was exposed, morale took a nosedive, and the company's stock plummeted.

AN INABILITY TO BE CONSISTENT IN MOODS, BEHAVIOR, ATTITUDES, POLICIES, AND DECISION-MAKING STYLE

A CEO, Cornelia, lounged on her couch and said to me, "I'm just tired. I don't want to do anything. I've been in this business for ten years and I'm exhausted. I can't stop now, but I'm emotionally depleted. Every time I think of what I have to do, I feel like a petulant child digging her heels in defiantly. The problem is, the person I'm defying is me!"

"Wait a minute," I cautioned. "Let's talk about the part that you are 'defying' and see what we find. Who are you resisting?"

"Well, Harriet, of course," was her emphatic reply.

"Who is Harriet?" I asked.

"Harriet is an internal voice of mine, a remnant of my perfectionistic mother. Harriet runs the show, and you better get out of her way. She's always on top of everything. Harriet wears a tailored suit with a high-necked blouse and comfortable low-heeled pumps. She is focused and on target with all her projects. She is organized, makes plans, looks ahead, and anticipates all possible outcomes. She has looked at the situation from all angles and is prepared for anything. She gets up early, and armed with her 'To Do' list she attacks the day with zeal. Harriet can make anything happen. She's the one who has built this business into what it is today. She's a winner!"

"How do you feel about Harriet?" I ventured.

"I hate her. No, I don't. She's important, but she drives me nuts. She makes me crazy with all of the demands she puts on me. She never lets me rest. Push a little harder, do just one more thing. Go ahead, you can do it," Cornelia said venomously.

"So tell me, where's Harriet these days?" I asked curiously.

"She's in the closet," Cornelia said. "I locked her there when I got back from the last business trip. *I* didn't, but this part of me that wants to relax did. It's the only way that I get any peace and quiet."

"What should we call the part of you that wants peace and quiet?" I asked.

"Jasmine," she said with conviction. "Jasmine is the one who couldn't care less about work. She's the one who just wants to be a mother and stay home and play with the children. Jasmine wants to smell the flowers, watch the sunsets, do jigsaw puzzles, and read stories to the boys. Jasmine hangs out in jeans and flannel shirts and doesn't even own a business suit. Her hair hangs loosely around her shoulders and her nails are never polished. She wears moccasins and is always smiling. Jasmine is content to let life deal its hand and enjoy every unstructured, unstressful moment."

I asked her if Jasmine was like anyone she had ever known. She replied, "Yes, she's calm, relaxed, and laid back just like my father. He never worried about anything, and took life just as it came."

It was clear to both of us that Jasmine and Harriet needed to get to know each other and ultimately become integrated. As it was, Jasmine would lock Harriet in the closet and run the show until Harriet broke out of her prison and ran roughshod over gentle Jasmine. She would take charge of anything that Jasmine let fall by the wayside. Harriet was usually furious when she finally burst out, because after Jasmine's neglect there was so much to do.

211

I wondered why the two parts of Cornelia were so separate, almost antithetical. When I asked her, she told me that it could be on account of the divorce between her parents. She felt that part of her mother was inside of her, and part of her father too, but that the two parts had never been integrated. Her loyalty to each prevented her from fully blending the two sides together.

Cornelia had to find a way to balance her two selves. She was a binary person who acted out certain traits from each of her parents but never really integrated them into her own personality. Since she had lived through a traumatic divorce, she felt internally divorced. She had to heal the internal schism between the two sides which emulated her two different parents, and blend them into one integrated, adult person. Otherwise, the shift between Harriet and Jasmine made Cornelia uncomfortable inside, and as a result her behavior was inconsistent and changeable from day to day.

RIGIDITY IN THINKING—A BINARY APPROACH TO PROBLEM-SOLVING

Jay was an interior designer in charge of all large industrial projects—hotels, resorts, and conference centers—for his firm. He was talented and respected by his peers. He had one tragic flaw: his people skills were very weak. At best he was judgmental and critical, and at worst he was argumentative, righteous, and downright abusive. When people came to him with questions and suggestions he was often closed to their ideas. He was unwilling for anyone else to be right. If he weren't so gifted at what he did management would have written him off, but he was too valuable to discard.

One day, Tom, one of his direct subordinates, came to him with a color scheme for a resort, and Jay's reaction was shock and horror at Tom's attempt at color coordination.

"What were you thinking of?" Jay said in amazement. "I thought we had discussed this at least three times. Where were you? Didn't you listen to what I said? Really, do I have to do everything myself?"

"I thought that peach, gray, and turquoise were the right combination for the southwestern motif. You said you wanted to juxtapose the earthtones with the colors of the nineties," Tom said.

"The gray is dull, boring, and makes businessmen feel like they're in an office instead of a resort. I told you we wanted them to forget about the office, leave their troubles downtown, and come to the worry-free world of our resort. Terra-cotta would have been a much better choice. Do it over!"

Jay was angry, contentious, abusive, and just plain mean. He was completely intolerant; worse, he was unforgiving. He all but said, "You idiot, you moron, you imbecile! You can't do anything right!"

Jay was now faced with a potential walk-out. After the incident, Tom complained to his colleagues. People were once again appalled by Jay's abusive behavior, and decided they would no longer put up with "Jay the Hun," as he was unlovingly called.

We were called in to work with Jay. His manager explained that he was too valuable as a creative genius to simply fire. On the other hand, his co-workers were afraid of him and dreaded their weekly meetings. Something had to be done. "We need to teach this guy how to work with people," Jerry, his boss, explained. "He's too valuable to us to let go, but he has the people skills of a Neanderthal. If you can't bring him around, we'll have to get rid of him. I don't want it to come to that. He's a talented guy, but he's causing more damage than he's worth. See what you can do. This is our last resort."

I set out on a mission to discover what drove Jay and where he learned his management style. The first thing I had to do was meet with Jay and see if he were aware of the general perception of him as a manager. I had to find out what he thought, what he felt, and what he wanted. Then I had to see if he would allow me to be his coach and develop his people skills.

Jay let me know that he was concerned about his staff being distant and unwilling to come to him with their problems. He couldn't see the relationship between his actions and their reactions. He felt misunderstood and unfairly accused. We used a questionnaire which his staff completed anonymously. When he heard the feedback, he was alarmed at the discrepancy between his reality and their perceptions. He started to consider that maybe everyone wasn't wrong, and that he might have something to learn. Jay was finally willing, so we set out to humanize him.

Jay's mother, Eleanor, was always beautifully dressed in stylish designer clothes. She payed inordinate attention to the details of her life. Her home was immaculate, and she ran a tight ship. She tolerated no ambiguity or uncertainty. Her husband, Ross, was the head of a world-renowned luxury hotel. Eleanor had to devote large portions of her life to entertaining clients and guests of the hotel. Although on the surface it looked as if Ross were in charge, Eleanor was the power behind the throne. Jay's father was a personable, charming, well-liked kind of guy. Without a mean bone in his body, and pleasant to a fault, he always had a kind word to say about everyone. When it came to decision-making, he usually acquiesced to Eleanor.

During his formative years, Jay watched his two parents closely. He saw his mother, who constantly made things happen, juxtaposed with his father, whose mild manner he rejected. He decided unconsciously to emulate his mother and to shun his father's sweetness. Jay became a caricature of his mother. He unconsciously incorporated all of Eleanor's strength, conviction, and decisiveness, but excluded her compassion, empathy, and gentleness, qualities which he associated with the rejected father.

Initially, Jay had been resistant to change, thinking that he was right and "they" were wrong. Together we had to transcend the right/wrong paradigm and build a more effective developmental model. As our conversations progressed, Jay grew more open to what didn't work about his behavior with other people. Deep down he cared about his staff and didn't want to hurt them with his looks, tone, and cryptic attitude.

Gradually, he opened up to the possibility that he could change his lifelong patterns and become a better manager, but it took time. His old behaviors were deeply ingrained, and letting go of them caused discomfort. He felt, in part, that he *was* his behaviors, and that if he let go of them he would no longer be who he was. Learning how to separate his identity from his behaviors was the first task at hand.

We began to coach him on how to handle interactions and situations in a more supportive and caring manner. We gave him private feedback after observing him conduct a staff meeting. We sat in on individual meetings with his designers, and then discussed them afterwards. He would talk to us about his reactions and find ways to communicate more effectively and in a less volatile fashion. The change didn't occur overnight, but with his willingness and commitment we brought about amazing results. Day by day, incident by incident, situation by situation, he learned alternative ways of dealing with people which were more effective than his distorted emulation of his mother.

COMPULSIVE BEHAVIOR: OVERLY PERFECTIONISTIC, CONSCIENTIOUS, ORDERLY, OR DRIVEN TOWARD ACHIEVEMENT

A certain organization offering individual human potential training and seminars was on a very fast track. Business doubled every month. The office environment was charged with electricity. The people who worked there were up-tempo, positive, and focused on getting the job done. They loved their jobs because they felt validated and able to make a contribution. It was a fun place to work, and its employees felt like a team.

Four times a year, a large presentation was produced which was the primary focus for everyone in the organization. Marilyn, one of the event's main managers, was in charge of Tracy. Tracy, a new volunteer, was a dedicated and good worker, but a rather slow one. She had a good heart, and had volunteered for the event because she believed in the organization and wanted to share in its positive energy. Tracy was lettering ten signs for the event, but was having some trouble getting all the letters lined up properly. She wasn't a graphic artist and wasn't particularly skilled in sign-painting, but nevertheless Marilyn decided that this was a good opportunity for her to learn. Tracy was feeling rather frustrated.

"I want those signs to be perfect," said Marilyn. "Not one letter out of place, got it?"

"I'm doing the best I can," said Tracy. "At this rate, it's going to take me all night."

"I don't care if you're up for the next three nights, these signs need to be perfect. I don't care if you sleep or not, that's not important to me. What is important is to have this event be perfect," Marilyn said with conviction. "I don't know if you've ever done anything perfectly in your whole life, but I want this event to be flawless, and it starts with the signs. This is your opportunity to go beyond your reasons and excuses and be the truly incredible person that you are. You can demonstrate that by making these signs perfectly."

"O.K., I've done five already. Can I go home, even if the rest are not done?" Tracy asked timidly.

"You're believing your own excuses. These are *your* signs. I want you to take total responsibility for them. These signs represent your life. These signs are you at this moment. If this was the last thing that you did in your life, would you want those signs to look like that? You see, it's not about getting the signs done, it's about the signs being an extension of you. When you put yourself one hundred percent into a project, and you give all of yourself, then you've done a hundred percent. There's nothing else to give. I want you to have the experience of doing something a hundred percent, maybe for the first time in your life. I want you to give up your reasons and excuses and give all you have to these signs. I want you to go beyond your limits, to do something magnificent and really surprise yourself. This is your chance to break through to a level of yourself that you didn't even know existed. The only way you're going to produce results is to press through your tiredness, your hunger, your whining, and find your own greatness," Marilyn said triumphantly.

Tracy was confused. It sounded like Marilyn was empowering her, but something was off about it. She was hearing one thing and feeling something else. She couldn't quite sort out whether she was being used or abused. It sounded good, but was she thinking clearly? Was she serving the organization, or was the organization taking advantage of her? If she told her mother about giving a hundred percent toward making the signs perfect, would she think she had totally lost her mind? Was this pursuit of excellence, or simple exploitation? Was this a new, more enlightened way of approaching work, through thoroughness and commitment, or was this a slick way of recruiting slave labor? Why did the words sound so good while she felt so strange inside?

This was a boundary issue for Tracy. There is a very fine line between being managed and supported and being manipulated and coerced. People from dysfunctional homes have difficulties determining what going a hundred percent is and what going over the edge is. Since their boundaries are porous, they have trouble ascertaining what their limits are. If you are motivated by the desire to be liked, then that need eclipses your ability to know when to stop. If the opinion of someone else is more important than your own, you will look to that person for approval, acceptance, validation, and love before you look to yourself. You will ignore your own signposts, and follow someone else's.

Marilyn came from a rigid background in which you did what you were told and didn't question authority. Her parents were German immigrants. Since she was the eldest, she absorbed the values which her parents transmitted to her. Her family had prepared her well for this situation. Her mother was very demanding, aggressive, and a relentless, take-charge person. She was a heavyset, impenetrable figure. Her father was timid, low-key, withdrawn, and compliant. Marilyn got points for getting things done, meeting expectations, and producing incredible results. As a result, she became almost machine-like in her demeanor. She fit well into the organizational culture and got the job done any way she could. She could be counted on, and she rose rapidly in the organization.

Tracy was a model child who was always rewarded for being good. She was the only child in a middle-class family. Her father worked for a money-management firm in New York, and her alcoholic mother stayed home. She decided early on that she needed to behave like the perfect child in order to stabilize the house. She believed that her mother's drinking was within her own control and that she had to do everything right in order to keep from upsetting anyone. She had an overdeveloped sense of responsibility and viewed all upsets and problems as her fault. This is typical behavior for an adult child of an alcoholic home. Tracy couldn't bear risking disapproval. She needed people to like her and care about her. She was afraid of being rejected and unloved. Her pattern complemented Marilyn's beautifully.

Like people, organizations have specific personalities. Sometimes dysfunctional behavior is localized and specific. It may occur between departments, divisions, or subgroups. It is important to know how to focus, detect, diagnose, and tackle situational negaholism in the work place.

The situation with the organization Marilyn and Tracy were involved in persisted until enough people had complained that it became obvious something was wrong. Management ended up softening its rigid stance somewhat, but the problem did not disappear entirely. The organization is to this day still not an easy environment to work in.

CHAPTER 9

◆

HOW TO
WORK WITH YOURSELF
AS A
NEGAHOLIC
IN THE
WORKPLACE

While reading this book, you may have identified
with some of the examples and stories. In addition to
recognizing some of the people with whom you work,
or have worked, you may also have thought, "That
description sounds just like me! I'd like to know what
to do about my own negaholism on the job." If you
have had this thought, then this chapter was designed
for you.

Here are some questions to help you determine if
you are a negaholic in the office:

1. Do you get anxious or feel extremely concerned
   when you think about promotion, rewards, massive layoffs, an acquisition, a company merger, or a
   buy-out?   YES ◇   NO ◇

221

2. Do you have difficulty saying, "No," or knowing when enough is enough? YES ◇ NO ◇

3. Do you have difficulty speaking up when you know something isn't right? YES ◇ NO ◇

4. Do you have a strong need to do things "your way," and insist on being left alone to do your work?
YES ◇ NO ◇

5. Do you take on the issues, problems, and concerns of the business as your own, to the point where it affects your health? YES ◇ NO ◇

6. Are you so eager to be included and belong that your compromise yourself or your values?
YES ◇ NO ◇

7. Do you find yourself having troubles with authority figures? YES ◇ NO ◇

8. Do you notice that the traumatic events in your personal life get in the way of doing your job?
YES ◇ NO ◇

9. Are you so loyal to your boss or co-workers that you would honor that loyalty over speaking up for your well-being, their personal health, or the health of the company? YES ◇ NO ◇

10. Are you more concerned about other employees and the company in general than you are about your own well-being? YES ◇ NO ◇

If you answered "Yes" to any one of these questions, read on; there are probably some important ideas in this last chapter that you need to think over.

ABANDONMENT

If you are afraid of being laid off, or not being promoted or if you often feel left out, unimportant, or forgotten, you may have a fear of abandonment. If this is the case, it is vital to:

State your concerns: Talk to your supervisor or manager and tell him or her what your concerns are. Ask if your worries are valid or if you are imagining things. Confirm or discount your suspicions and fears. Gather the facts from the most reliable source. Record what you find out, and refer to it when you get nervous.

State your needs: After you have the facts, then you can state your needs. You will want to communicate without appearing frail, frantic, or paranoid. For instance: "I am concerned that because of the reorganization I might be out of a job. These concerns run very deep for me because I have a high need for security. I would like you to level with me. If I need to go out and start looking for a job, I would appreciate you being really honest with me so that I can prepare myself and plan for the future. This will help me either to continue to do my job or come to terms with the potential reality with which I am preoccupied." If you trust your manager, this type of communication should help. If you don't trust you immediate boss, find someone you do trust.

Gather all the available data: When you go to meetings, receive memos, or have conversations with associates, pay attention to the available information. Ask questions and pursue your most reliable sources. Beware of listening to third-party communications which may have become distorted in the retelling. Also watch out for rumors and gossip which plant the seeds of needless concern. Stick with the facts, and check out everything else.

Self-management: If you notice that you start having conversations with yourself inside your head, pay attention. Write down what the voices are saying and see if you can determine whose voice is talking to you. Whatever the voice says, agree with it. The voices from the mind have amassed data which is usually accurate, so don't bother refuting them. Agree, and then ask yourself what you want to do about the situation. Externalize the thoughts in your head, then look at them squarely and decide how to proceed.

CONTROL

If you are afraid of change, of being out of control, of others controlling you, or if you have a need to control or dominate others, you probably have a problem regarding control. If so, here's what to do: In any given situation, ask yourself what is the worst that could happen if you lost control, and if you could survive it.

If you need to always be in control, ask yourself if you could let someone else be in control for once, just to try on a new behavior. Experiment with doing nothing and see what happens. If everyone survives, then you know it wasn't that terrible. Get a coloring book and color outside the lines. Give yourself permission to relinquish control, to be imperfect, to break the rules. Experiment by breaking some harmless rules. Have breakfast at dinnertime, or eat dessert at the beginning of your meal. I'm not advocating breaking the law or hurting anyone, but breaking harmless rules helps control-dominated people break their habit.

BOUNDARIES

If you have trouble saying "No," if you're a workaholic, if you put yourself last, if you often feel overwhelmed or run-down, then you definitely have a boundary issue.

Constructing boundaries is an interesting and challenging task. You must differentiate between boundaries and barriers. A boundary is a tool which helps you define yourself. With no boundaries, you have no definition, no identity; you simply merge into everything and everyone with whom you interact. A boundary can be physical, like your property line or the perimeters of your neighborhood. A boundary can be interpersonal, for instance what you will and won't tolerate. A boundary can be a personal policy which states what works for you and what you require to be fully functional and healthy.

In a work environment, for instance, you may need to stipulate that you are hypoglycemic and need small snacks eight times a day. You may communicate that you need to leave the office at five on Thursdays to go to your son's soccer practice. You may need to demand that the first fifteen minutes or half-hour of each day are to be "your" time, totally undisturbed, so that you can handle the accumulation of paperwork. You may declare the time between one and two as "return-call-hour" in which you want no interruptions. Establishing boundaries is healthy. Saying you'll do whatever is needed and wanted is a wonderful gesture, but it invites situations which yield later resentments. It is much more important to be clear about what you will do and what you won't do.

DENIAL

If you find yourself making excuses for others, always putting on rose-tinted glasses, giving people the benefit of the doubt to the point of extremes, and looking the other way, then you may be denying the reality of a situation.

If denial is your weakness, then you could probably use the help of others. Denial is slippery because if you're good at it you'll never even know you're doing it. This is where others come into the picture. Without making them into co-dependents, you could choose one or two people whom you really trust to be your "monitors of the truth." First make a pact with those you trust and ask them for feedback on your behavior. Tell them that you don't want to deny the reality of a situation, and that you want them to help you see situations and people as they really are, not as you would like them to be. If these people are work associates, then they can help you on the job.

INDEPENDENCE/DEPENDENCE

If you always feel the need to work alone, to do things your way, to be unsupervised, if you find it difficult to receive feedback, to hear that you are wrong, or to depend on others for support, resources, or information, then you may have a problem in this area.

This is one of those areas where trying on a new behavior will feel as uncomfortable as trying on someone else's shoes. The behavior you want to try on is asking for support. First of all, prime the people from whom you are going to ask support. Tell them how difficult it is for you, and that you are going to initiate a new behavior. Post signs around your office which say, "Reach Out," "People Are Here to Support You," or "You Deserve Support." Put a red dot on your phone to remind you that you don't have to do it all alone. When you feel all alone and start to muscle through, remind yourself that you can ask for what you need.

RESPONSIBILITY/IRRESPONSIBILITY

If you hold yourself responsible for concerns and issues within the company which are way beyond your position or authority, or if you find yourself shying away from any responsibility for fear of being blamed, or doing the minimum in order to just get by, you may have a problem in this area.

If you are overly responsible, you need to allow yourself to be irresponsible. I'm not referring to paying the rent, caring for your children, or feeding the dog. I am referring to your responsibilities in the office. This sounds like a capital offense, but the truth of the matter is that the only way to get back in balance is to swing the pendulum in the opposite direction—to "unstick" the behavior pattern. Try answering the phone after the third ring rather than after the first; if you usually answer it after the third, try the first. Try going home at six o'clock rather than staying until eight; if you always go home as soon as you can bolt out the door, then try staying late just to change the pattern. Try giving yourself permission to get your expense report done either early or late, breaking whatever pattern you have mechanically locked into.

THE NEED TO BE LIKED

If you hate people to say "No" to you, and more than anything want to be accepted, approved of, included, and loved, if you will compromise yourself in order to win someone over, then you certainly have difficulties in this area.

First you have to go through the uncomfortable process of examining whether or not you are willing to be yourself, honor your values, and be willing for the world to hate you. This is too large a task for someone who has spent the majority of his or her life wanting others' approval, acceptance, validation, and love. Results in this area only occur in small increments. Asking for any radical change in the area of wanting to be liked is like asking for a miracle. The change is too radical. Take it slowly, and ask yourself, "Would I be willing to consider risking disapproval in this situation?" This is as much as you can deal with at one time. If the answer is "Yes," go for it and take the risk. If the answer is "No," then do nothing and notice what happens. Don't berate or judge yourself, just notice what you do and take note of it. Some day in the future you may have the courage to stand up for what you believe in, to risk disapproval. When you do, you'll know that you are a different person.

AUTHORITY ISSUES

If you have a push-pull relationship with your managers or find yourself rebelling as a matter of course, if you are suspicious of authorities or resistant to their requests, then you probably have a problem with authority.

If you have any reactions to authority figures, try this behavior on for size: for a whole day, when your boss asks you to do something don't question it or try to understand it, just do it. Another thing you can do is to make your boss right. Whatever she says, she is right for a whole day. This means that even if she is wrong, you still make her right.

THE NEED FOR EXCITEMENT, DRAMA, AND CHAOS

Adrenaline runs the dysfunctional home, and so the negaholic employee is often in search of the adrenaline rush which enables him to feel alive and vital.

Ask yourself what would life be like if there were no emergencies, no traumas, no crises. Ask yourself if you would be willing to experience boredom. Try on a day with no adrenaline. See how it feels. It will probably feel pretty bland in comparison to the high level of drama you have experienced. Give yourself permission to go to the movies, to watch soap operas, to read romantic novels. Let yourself get the adrenaline rush vicariously, from watching others, rather than from having to be the lead in your own real-life soap opera.

LOYALTIES

People from dysfunctional homes display extreme loyalty. If you are loyal to the point that you are blind to dysfunctional realities, then being too loyal is one of your problems. Loyalty to an unhealthy boss or organization will not serve you in the long run.

Ask yourself to whom are you loyal, then answer the question. Ask yourself to whom you are so loyal that you would put yourself at risk, then answer that question. Then ask yourself which of your loyalties are healthy and which ones are unhealthy. After you sort out the healthy loyalties from the unhealthy ones, then ask yourself what you are willing to do about the unhealthy ones. Write down your strategy, see what comes out, then put a date on it and go for everything you can possibly imagine.

CONCLUSION

There are negaholic individuals, departments, and companies. There are unhealthy environments which cause stress and dysfunction. There are also healthy companies which are committed to putting out good products and services, and which contribute to the well-being of people and the environment.

You can't change the whole world, and you certainly can't change other people, but you do have the ability to change yourself. You can have a positive impact on your job, the people with whom you work, and the entire company. If you decide today that you want to be a functioning, healthy individual who brings health to those whose lives you touch, you can make a profound difference with every interaction. You can begin the process of eliminating negaholism with each contact. The choice is up to you.

If you would like more information on licensing, consulting, training, speaking, curriculum design, train-the-trainer, facilitation, or transforming negative corporate cultures in the areas of:

Visioning
Managing organizational change
Team building
Customer service
Management development
    Interviewing
    Performance appraisal
    Employee orientation
    Stress management
    Communication
    Conflict management
    Dealing with difficult employees
    Delegation
    Goal setting
    How to run meetings
    Interviewing skills
    Presentation skills
    Sales training
    Stress management
    Telephone courtesy
    Time management

Please call 1-800-321-NEGA or write:

The MMS Institute
P.O. Box 30052
Santa Barbara, CA
93130-0052

ABOUT THE AUTHOR

◆

CHÉRIE CARTER-SCOTT is an entrepreneur, lecturer, seminar leader, trainer, TV-show host, and chairman of the board of the MMS Institute, a human and organizational development firm specializing in personal and professional transformation. She has worked with more than ten thousand people in workshops and private consultation all over the world. She conducts workshops and trainings in Holland and Switzerland as well as in the U.S. Her corporate clients include IBM, GTE/GTEL, Burger King, AMI, First Interstate Bank, Chevron, and American Express. She lives with her sister/business partner and her daughter in Santa Barbara and in Holland.